Language: Usage and Practice, Grade 8

Contents

W9-CFK-104

Introduction...3
Skills Correlation.......................................5
Assessment...7

Unit 1: Vocabulary

Synonyms and Antonyms.......................11
Homonyms..12
Homographs...13
Prefixes...14
Suffixes...15
Contractions..16
Compound Words....................................17
Connotation/Denotation..........................18
Idioms...19
Unit 1 Test...20

Unit 2: Sentences

Recognizing Sentences...........................22
Types of Sentences.................................23
Complete Subjects and Predicates.........24
Simple Subjects and Predicates.............25
Position of Subjects.................................26
Compound Subjects and Predicates.......27
Combining Sentences.............................28
Direct Objects...29
Indirect Objects......................................30
Independent and Subordinate Clauses...31
Adjective and Adverb Clauses................32
Compound and Complex Sentences........33
Correcting Run-on Sentences.................35
Expanding Sentences.............................36
Unit 2 Test...37

Unit 3: Grammar and Usage

Common and Proper Nouns.....................39
Concrete, Abstract, and Collective Nouns........40
Singular and Plural Nouns......................41
Possessive Nouns..................................43
Appositives...44
Verbs...45
Verb Phrases..46
Verb Tenses..47
Using Irregular Verbs.............................48
More Irregular Verbs..............................50
Even More Irregular Verbs.....................52
Mood...53
Transitive and Intransitive Verbs...........54
Active and Passive Voice.......................56
Gerunds..57
Infinitives..58
Participles...59
Using *Lie/Lay*..60
Using *Sit/Set* and *Learn/Teach*.........61
Pronouns..62
Using *Its* and *It's*...............................63
Demonstrative and Indefinite Pronouns...........64
Antecedents..65
Relative Pronouns..................................66
Using *Who/Whom*.................................67
Using Pronouns......................................68
Adjectives...69
Demonstrative Adjectives.......................71
Comparing with Adjectives.....................72
Adverbs...73
Comparing with Adverbs........................74
Using Adjectives and Adverbs...............75
Prepositions and Prepositional Phrases...........76
Conjunctions...78
Double Negatives....................................79
Unit 3 Test...80

Contents continued

Contents *continued*

Unit 4: Capitalization and Punctuation

Using Capital Letters 82
Using End Punctuation 84
Using Commas 86
Using Quotation Marks and Apostrophes 88
Using Colons and Semicolons 89
Using Other Punctuation 90
Unit 4 Test 91

Unit 5: Composition

Writing Sentences 93
Writing Paragraphs 94
Writing Topic Sentences 95
Writing Supporting Details 96
Topic and Audience 97
Brainstorming 98
Outlining 99
Persuasive Composition 100
Revising and Proofreading 102
Unit 5 Test 104

Unit 6: Study Skills

Dictionary: Syllables 106
Dictionary: Definitions and Parts of
  Speech 107
Dictionary: Etymologies 108
Using the Library 109
Using an Encyclopedia 110
Using an Encyclopedia Index 111
Using a Thesaurus 112
Using an Atlas 113
Using an Almanac 114
Choosing Reference Sources 115
Using Reference Sources 116
Unit 6 Test 118

Answer Key 120
Language Terms .... Inside Back Cover

The *Language: Usage and Practice* series meets many needs.

- It is designed for students who require additional practice in the basics of effective writing and speaking.
- It provides focused practice in key grammar, usage, mechanics, and composition areas.
- It helps students gain ownership of essential skills.
- It presents practice exercises in a clear, concise format in a logical sequence.
- It allows for easy and independent use.

The *Language: Usage and Practice* lessons are organized into a series of units arranged in a logical sequence.

- vocabulary
- sentences
- grammar and usage
- mechanics of capitalization and punctuation
- composition skills

The *Language: Usage and Practice* lessons are carefully formatted for student comfort.

- Systematic, focused attention is given to just one carefully selected skill at a time.
- Rules are clearly stated at the beginning of each lesson and are illustrated with examples.
- Key terms are introduced in bold type.
- Meaningful practice exercises reinforce the skill.
- Each lesson is clearly labeled, and directions are clear and uncomplicated.

The *Language: Usage and Practice* series stresses the application of language principles in a variety of ways.

- Students are asked to match, circle, or underline elements in a predetermined sentence.
- Students are also asked to use what they have learned in an original sentence or in rewriting a sentence.

The *Language: Usage and Practice* series is designed for independent use.

- ☐ Because the format is logical and consistent and the vocabulary is carefully controlled, students can use *Language: Usage and Practice* with a high degree of independence.
- ☐ Copies of the worksheets can be given to individuals, pairs of students, or small groups for completion.
- ☐ Worksheets can be used in the language arts center.
- ☐ Worksheets can be given as homework for reviewing and reinforcing skills.

The *Language: Usage and Practice* series provides writing instruction.

- ☐ The process approach to teaching writing provides success for most students.
- ☐ *Language: Usage and Practice* provides direct support for the teaching of composition and significantly enhances those strategies and techniques commonly associated with the process-writing approach.
- ☐ Each book includes a composition unit that provides substantial work with composition skills, such as writing topic sentences, selecting supporting details, taking notes, writing reports, and revising and proofreading.
- ☐ Also included in the composition unit is practice with various prewriting activities, such as clustering and brainstorming, which play an important part in process writing.
- ☐ The composition lessons are presented in the same rule-plus-practice format as in the other units.

The *Language: Usage and Practice* series includes additional features.

- ☐ **Unit Tests**   Use the unit tests to check student progress and prepare students for standardized tests.
- ☐ **Sequential Support**   The content of each unit is repeated and expanded in subsequent levels as highlighted in the skills correlation chart on pages 5 and 6.
- ☐ **Assessment**   Use the Assessment on pages 7–10 to determine the skills your students need to practice.
- ☐ **Language Terms**   Provide each student with a copy of the list of language terms on the inside back cover to keep for reference throughout the year.
- ☐ **Small-Group Activities**   Use the worksheets as small-group activities to give students the opportunity to work cooperatively.

The *Language: Usage and Practice* series is a powerful tool!

The activities use a variety of strategies to maintain student interest. Watch your students' language improve as skills are applied in structured, relevant practice!

Skills Correlation

	1	2	3	4	5	6	7	8	High School
Vocabulary									
Rhyming Words	■	■							
Synonyms and Antonyms	■	■	■	■	■	■	■		
Homonyms	■	■	■	■	■	■	■	■	
Multiple Meanings/Homographs	■	■	■	■	■	■	■	■	
Prefixes and Suffixes		■	■	■	■	■	■	■	
Compound Words		■	■	■	■	■	■		
Contractions		■	■	■	■	■	■		
Idioms									
Connotation/Denotation					■	■	■	■	
Sentences									
Word Order in Sentences	■	■		■					
Recognizing Sentences and Sentence Types	■	■	■	■	■	■	■	■	
Subjects and Predicates	■	■	■	■	■	■	■	■	
Compound/Complex Sentences			■	■	■	■	■		
Sentence Combining		■	■	■	■	■	■		
Run-on Sentences			■	■	■	■	■		
Independent and Subordinate Clauses							■	■	
Compound Subjects and Predicates	■				■	■	■	■	
Direct and Indirect Objects						■	■	■	
Inverted Word Order						■	■	■	
Grammar and Usage									
Common and Proper Nouns	■	■	■	■	■	■	■	■	
Singular and Plural Nouns	■	■	■	■	■	■	■	■	
Possessive Nouns			■	■	■	■	■	■	
Appositives									
Verbs and Verb Tense	■	■	■	■	■	■	■	■	
Regular/Irregular Verbs	■	■	■	■	■	■	■	■	
Subject/Verb Agreement	■	■	■	■	■	■	■	■	
Verb Phrases						■	■	■	
Transitive and Intransitive Verbs							■	■	
Verbals: Gerunds, Participles, and Infinitives							■	■	
Active and Passive Voice							■	■	
Mood								■	
Pronouns	■	■	■	■	■	■	■	■	
Antecedents						■	■	■	
Articles	■	■	■		■	■			
Adjectives	■	■	■	■	■	■	■	■	
Correct Word Usage (e.g., may/can, sit/set)	■		■	■		■	■		
Adverbs			■	■	■	■	■	■	
Prepositions					■	■	■		
Prepositional Phrases					■	■	■		
Conjunctions					■	■	■		
Interjections						■	■		
Double Negatives							■	■	
Capitalization and Punctuation									
Capitalization: First Word in Sentence	■	■	■	■		■	■		
Capitalization: Proper Nouns	■	■	■	■	■	■	■	■	
Capitalization: in Letters			■	■	■		■	■	
Capitalization: Abbreviations and Titles			■	■	■	■	■	■	
Capitalization: Proper Adjectives					■	■	■	■	

Skills Correlation
Language: Usage and Practice 8, SV 1419027859

	1	2	3	4	5	6	7	8	High School
Capitalization and Punctuation (cont'd)									
End Punctuation	■	■	■	■	■	■	■	■	■
Commas		■	■	■	■	■	■	■	■
Apostrophes in Contractions		■	■	■	■	■	■	■	
Apostrophes in Possessives			■	■	■	■	■	■	
Quotation Marks			■	■	■	■	■	■	
Colons/Semicolons						■	■	■	■
Hyphens									
Composition									
Expanding Sentences				■		■	■	■	
Paragraphs: Topic Sentence (main idea)		■	■	■	■	■	■	■	
Paragraphs: Supporting Details		■	■	■	■	■	■	■	
Order in Paragraphs				■	■	■	■		
Writing Process:									
Audience				■		■	■		
Topic			■	■			■		
Outlining				■			■		
Clustering/Brainstorming						■	■		
Note Taking							■		
Revising/Proofreading						■	■		
Types of Writing:									
Poem	■								
Letter	■	■	■			■			
"How-to" Paragraph				■					
Invitation				■					
Telephone Message				■					
Conversation					■				
Narrative Paragraph					■				
Comparing and Contrasting						■			
Descriptive Paragraph						■			
Report							■		
Interview								■	
Persuasive Composition								■	
Readiness/Study Skills									
Grouping	■		■						
Letters of Alphabet	■								
Listening	■	■							
Making Comparisons	■	■							
Organizing Information		■	■						
Following Directions	■	■	■	■	■				
Alphabetical Order	■	■	■	■	■				
Using a Dictionary:									
Definitions		■	■			■	■	■	
Guide Words/Entry Words		■	■	■	■	■	■	■	
Syllables and Pronunciation						■	■	■	
Multiple Meanings		■	■			■	■	■	
Word Origins						■	■	■	
Parts of a Book		■					■		
Using the Library						■	■	■	
Using Encyclopedias				■	■	■	■		
Using Reference Books						■	■	■	
Using the *Readers' Guide*							■	■	
Using Tables, Charts, Graphs, and Diagrams							■	■	
Choosing Appropriate Sources							■	■	

www.harcourtschoolsupply.com

Skills Correlation
Language: Usage and Practice 8, SV 1419027859

Name _____ Date _____

Assessment

✳ **Write S before each pair of synonyms, A before each pair of antonyms, and H before each pair of homonyms.**

_____ **1.** aloud, allowed   _____ **3.** argumentative, agreeable

_____ **2.** tiny, miniature   _____ **4.** massive, giant

✳ **Write the homograph for the pair of meanings.**

5. _____ **a.** to move slowly   **b.** a unit of measurement

✳ **Write P before each word with a prefix, S before each word with a suffix, and C before each compound word.**

_____ **6.** wishful   _____ **8.** unruly

_____ **7.** overblown   _____ **9.** misinform

✳ **Write the words that make up each contraction.**

10. they've _____ _____   **11.** we'll _____

✳ **Underline the word in parentheses that has the more positive connotation.**

12. The (generous, pushy) baker insisted we try the hot cookies.

✳ **Circle the letter of the idiom that means depressed.**

13. a. down in the dumps   **b.** in the doghouse

✳ **Write D before the declarative sentence, IM before the imperative sentence, E before the exclamatory sentence, and IN before the interrogative sentence. Then underline the simple subject and circle the simple predicate in each sentence.**

_____ **14.** Look out for that hole!   _____ **16.** Why are you still here?

_____ **15.** Please hand me the towel.   _____ **17.** I usually leave at noon.

✳ **Write CS before the sentence that has a compound subject and CP before the sentence that has a compound predicate.**

_____ **18.** Peaches and strawberries are great in pies.

_____ **19.** We watched and cheered our team.

✳ **Write CS before the compound sentence, RO before the run-on sentence, and I before the sentence that is in inverted order.**

_____ **20.** You have a toothache, you should go to the dentist.

_____ **21.** I wanted chocolate, but they only had vanilla.

_____ **22.** Up the tree scampered the squirrel.

✳ **Put brackets around the subordinate clause and underline the independent clause in this complex sentence. Then write DO above the direct object.**

23. The doctor handed Jesse the prescription that he needed.

Assessment, p. 2

❋ Underline the common nouns and circle the proper nouns in the sentence.

24. Ms. Chang rounded up the group and began the tour of the Jefferson Memorial.

❋ Circle the appositive in the sentence. Underline the noun it identifies or explains.

25. My favorite uncle, Tom Fiske, was recently elected mayor of Greenville.

❋ Write past, present, or future to show the tense of each underlined verb.

_____ 26. Kayti painted one wall in her kitchen pale blue.

_____ 27. Pete will call tomorrow morning at eight o'clock.

_____ 28. Each morning before breakfast, Juan walks two miles.

_____ 29. I will go to the library today.

❋ Circle the correct verbs in parentheses to complete each sentence.

30. There (is, are) only six weeks left before we (go, went) on vacation.

31. Steve (set, sat) down and (lay, laid) the sleeping kitten in his lap.

32. To (teach, learn) how to ski, you should (take, took) lessons.

33. (Sit, Set) the plate beside the sink where the glasses are (sitting, setting).

❋ Circle the letter of the sentence that is in the active voice.

34. a. The packages were sent two weeks ago.

   b. Phillip leaped to his feet to disagree with the speaker.

❋ Write SP before the sentence that has a subject pronoun, OP before the sentence that has an object pronoun, PP before the sentence that has a possessive pronoun, and IP before the sentence that has an indefinite pronoun. Circle the pronoun in each sentence.

_____ 35. Nobody understands what happened.   _____ 37. The horse raised its head to look at the dog.

_____ 36. Ella played the first song for him.   _____ 38. He sent the memo to four people.

❋ Underline the pronoun. Circle its antecedent.

39. Janet and Jason met to discuss the response to their request.

❋ Write adjective or adverb to describe the underlined word.

_____ 40. These days are the best of the summer.

_____ 41. Charlotte tiptoed quietly past the open door.

_____ 42. That was the most difficult skating move I've ever seen.

_____ 43. I really like Canadian bacon on my pizza.

_____ 44. The dachshund is a tiny breed of dog.

_____ 45. That heavy tree will be extremely hard to move.

❋ Underline each prepositional phrase twice. Circle each preposition. Underline the conjunction once.

46. I don't have the time or the patience to talk about the complaints of those people.

Name _____   Date _____

Assessment, p. 3

✻ **Rewrite the letter. Use capital letters and punctuation marks where needed.**

47.
591 w franklin place
bent tree tx 78709
jan 27 2007

dear ms coleman

    please know that I called you at exactly 915 but nobody answered the phone ____ i hope that youll allow me another opportunity to tell you about my work ____ i have exciting news ____ i won the national photo contest and my picture will be in the next issue of parks of the world

    i look forward to speaking with you ____ please call anytime this week between 1000 and 230 ____ ill be in one of these places my home my office or my car you have all three numbers ____

sincerely
eric flannery

_____

_____

_____

_____

_____

_____

_____

_____

✻ **Number the sentences in order with the topic sentence first.**

48. _____ Then they walk to find water, and they drink their fill.

49. _____ An elephant herd walks and eats most of the day.

50. _____ The herd wakes early to graze before it gets too hot.

51. _____ Finally, they lie down and sleep.

✻ **Write brainstorming, outlining, or persuading to describe each of the following.**

52. organizing your thoughts before you write _____

53. convincing others to accept a personal opinion _____

54. bringing to mind as many ideas as possible _____

Assessment, p. 4

✳ **Rewrite the sentence below. Correct the errors in the sentence by following the proofreader's marks.**

55. the movie began crowd the grew silent and and consentraited on the actshun

_____

✳ **Use the dictionary entry to answer the questions.**

honor (än´ ər) *n.* **1.** esteem; respect. **2.** recognition [Old French *honor*]

n.	noun	*v.*	verb	*adv.*	adverb
pron.	pronoun	*adj.*	adjective	*prep.*	preposition

56. What part of speech is the word <u>honor</u>? _____

57. Would <u>honest</u> come before or after <u>honor</u>? _____

58. Which language is in the history of the word <u>honor</u>? _____

59. Write <u>honor</u> separated into syllables. _____

✳ **Write the letter of the reference source on the line before its description.**

_____ 60. used to find synonyms and antonyms   **a.** dictionary

_____ 61. lists articles in magazines by author and subject   **b.** thesaurus

_____ 62. used to find definitions, pronunciations, and origins of words   **c.** encyclopedia

_____ 63. presents information about geographical locations   **d.** atlas

_____ 64. contains specific yearly information on a variety of topics   **e.** *Readers' Guide*

_____ 65. a source of articles about many different people and things   **f.** almanac

✳ **Write the call number group in which you would find each book.**

000–099 Reference	500–599 Science and Math
100–199 Philosophy	600–699 Technology
200–299 Religion	700–799 The Arts
300–399 Social Sciences	800–899 Literature
400–499 Languages	900–999 History and Geography

_____ 66. *Mathematics Made Easy*

_____ 67. *The Encyclopedia of Customs and Traditions*

_____ 68. *Learn Spanish While You Sleep*

_____ 69. *Modern Painters*

_____ 70. *Favorite Poems for Young People*

Name _____ Date _____

Synonyms and Antonyms

> • A **synonym** is a word that has the same or nearly the same meaning as one or more other words.
>   EXAMPLES: sick—ill   sad—unhappy

 Write a synonym for each word below.

1. discover _____   4. weary _____   7. capable _____

2. ridiculous _____   5. beautiful _____   8. funny _____

3. difficult _____   6. inquire _____   9. honest _____

 Rewrite the following sentences, using synonyms for the underlined words.

10. The <u>vacant</u> lot became the neighborhood playground.

_____

11. His broken leg slowly began to <u>mend</u>.

_____

12. The Barkers returned from their trip <u>weary</u> but happy.

_____

13. The energetic dog <u>bounded</u> across the lawn.

_____

> • An **antonym** is a word that has the opposite meaning of another word.
>   EXAMPLES: high—low   giant—tiny

 Write an antonym for each word below.

14. graceful _____   17. hastily _____   20. definite _____

15. difficult _____   18. deflate _____   21. superior _____

16. generous _____   19. valuable _____   22. abundance _____

 For each underlined word, underline the correct antonym in the parentheses.

23. Her <u>failure</u> was no surprise to those who knew her well.   (success, defeat)

24. Dr. Fenton always has a <u>mean</u> greeting for her patients.   (sarcastic, friendly)

25. His <u>cowardly</u> actions went unnoticed.   (courageous, fearful)

26. Our car is old and <u>dependable</u>.   (valuable, unreliable)

27. His <u>vague</u> answer cleared up the misunderstanding.   (rambling, specific)

Language: Usage and Practice 8, SV 1419027859

Name _____ Date _____

Homonyms

> • A **homonym** is a word that sounds the same as another word but has a different spelling and a different meaning.
>   EXAMPLES: their—they're—there   hear—here

 Underline the correct homonym in parentheses to complete each sentence.

1. What is the (weight, wait) of that rocket?

2. The (sale, sail) on the lake will be rough today.

3. Don't you like to (brows, browse) around in a bookstore?

4. We spent several (days, daze) at an old-fashioned (in, inn).

5. The ship was caught in an ice (flow, floe).

6. A large (boulder, bolder) rolled down the mountainside.

7. Why is that crowd on the (pier, peer)?

8. They asked the bank for a (lone, loan).

9. We drove four miles in a foggy (missed, mist).

10. Don't you like to (sea, see) a field of golden wheat?

11. Jack (threw, through) the ball (threw, through) the garage window.

12. We (buy, by) our fish from the market down on the (beach, beech).

13. The band will march down the middle (aisle, isle) of the auditorium.

14. Who is the (principal, principle) of your school?

15. The United States Congress (meats, meets) in the Capitol in Washington, D.C.

16. The farmer caught the horse by the (rain, reign, rein).

17. She stepped on the (break, brake) suddenly.

18. (Their, There) are too many people on this boat.

19. The wren (flew, flue) in a (strait, straight) line.

20. We were not (allowed, aloud) to visit the museum yesterday.

 Write a homonym for each word below.

21. weigh _____ 27. ate _____ 33. see _____

22. steal _____ 28. vain _____ 34. sent _____

23. sail _____ 29. strait _____ 35. pare _____

24. fare _____ 30. threw _____ 36. peace _____

25. maid _____ 31. soar _____ 37. sun _____

26. deer _____ 32. bored _____ 38. blue _____

Language: Usage and Practice 8, SV 1419027859

Homographs

> • A **homograph** is a word that has the same spelling as another word but a different meaning and sometimes a different pronunciation.
> EXAMPLE: <u>base</u>, meaning "the bottom on which a statue stands," and <u>base</u>, meaning "mean and selfish"

 Write the homograph for each pair of meanings below.

1. **a.** a large animal   **b.** to support or carry   _____

2. **a.** a person who jumps   **b.** a type of dress   _____

3. **a.** a cutting tool   **b.** the past tense of <u>see</u>   _____

4. **a.** to hit   **b.** a sweetened beverage   _____

5. **a.** silent   **b.** a type of flower   _____

6. **a.** a glass container   **b.** to rattle or shake   _____

7. **a.** a round object   **b.** a formal dance   _____

8. **a.** a part of the eye   **b.** a student   _____

 Write a homograph from the box to complete each sentence.

ball	jumper	punch	mum
bear	saw	jar	pupil

9. Jim and I _____ that movie last week.

10. The pitcher threw the _____ to home plate.

11. Joan's new _____ fit her very well.

12. Sharpen that _____ before you cut the wood.

13. That yellow _____ is the prettiest flower in the vase.

14. Jerry made a delicious _____ for the party.

15. The _____ was filled with strawberry jam.

16. The new _____ made new friends in school.

17. That _____ had two cubs yesterday.

18. My parents attended a formal _____ at the country club.

Name _____ Date _____

Name _____ Date

Prefixes

> - A **prefix** added to the beginning of a base word changes the meaning of the word.
>   EXAMPLE: in, meaning "not," + the base word visible = invisible, meaning "not visible"
>
> | EXAMPLES: | prefix | meaning | prefix | meaning |
> |---|---|---|---|---|
> | | in | not | re | again |
> | | dis | not | fore | before |
> | | un | not | mis | wrong |
> | | im | not | co | together |
> | | il | not, non | pre | before |

 On the line after each sentence, write a new word that means the same as the two underlined words combined. Use prefixes from the examples above. Use a dictionary if needed.

1. Shera was asked to write her report again. _____

2. At first, Shera was not pleased with the idea. _____

3. Then she remembered that the instructor had warned the class before that

   handwriting must be neat. _____

4. Shera looked at her paper and realized that it was not possible to read some

   of the words. _____

5. "I am not certain myself what the last sentence says," she thought. _____

6. "Did I spell that word wrong?" she wondered. _____

7. Shera realized that she tended to be not patient about her work. _____

 Add a prefix from the examples above to each word to make a new word. Then write the new word on the line.

8. read _____ 15. obey _____

9. pure _____ 16. match _____

10. wrap _____ 17. view _____

11. understand _____ 18. locate _____

12. mature _____ 19. fortune _____

13. arrange _____ 20. pay _____

14. equal _____ 21. fair _____

Name _____   Date _____

Suffixes

> • A **suffix** added to the end of a base word changes the meaning of the word.
>   EXAMPLE: <u>ward</u>, meaning "toward," + the base word <u>west</u> = <u>westward</u>, meaning "toward the west"
> • Sometimes you need to change the spelling of a base word when a suffix is added.
>   EXAMPLE: imagine—imagination

EXAMPLES:	suffix	meaning	suffix	meaning
	less	without	en	to make
	ish	of the nature of	ist	one skilled in
	ous	full of	able	able to be
	er	one who does	tion	art of
	hood	state of being	ful	full of
	ward	in the direction of	al	pertaining to
	ness	quality of	ible	able to be
	ment	act or process of	like	similar to

 Add a suffix from the examples above to each base word in parentheses. Write the new word in the sentence.

1. Kito wants to be a _____. (paint)

2. He is _____, working after school to earn money for art lessons.   (tire)

3. People say that his portraits are very _____. (life)

4. His talent as an _____ was apparent at an early age. (art)

5. In kindergarten his teacher noticed his _____ understanding of shapes and forms.   (remark)

6. She gave Kito a great deal of freedom and _____ (encourage)

7. Kito had a _____ for color. (fascinate)

8. Throughout his _____, he entered many contests and competitions.   (child)

9. His friends expect that he will become a _____ artist.   (fame)

 Add a suffix from the examples above to each root word. Then write the new word on the line.

10. rely _____

11. glory _____

12. color _____

13. occasion _____

14. fate _____

15. comfort _____

16. hope _____

17. believe _____

Language: Usage and Practice 8, SV 1419027859

Contractions

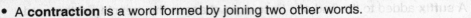

- A **contraction** is a word formed by joining two other words.
- An **apostrophe** shows where a letter or letters have been left out.
  EXAMPLE: he would = he'd
- Won't is an exception.
  EXAMPLE: will not = won't

 Write a sentence in which you use a contraction for each pair of words below.

1. I am _____

2. is not _____

3. do not _____

4. where is _____

5. should not _____

6. was not _____

7. were not _____

8. we will _____

9. they are _____

10. I have _____

Underline the contractions in the sentences below. Then write the two words that make up each contraction.

11. Jon and Janna won't be home until dinnertime. _____

12. Let's surprise them by having dinner ready. _____

13. Yes, that's a great idea. _____

14. I don't know what to cook. _____

15. I think we'd better have spaghetti. _____

16. Yes, we can't fail with that. _____

17. It's Jon's favorite. _____

18. Besides, you're the best spaghetti cook in the family. _____

19. We'll have so much fun! _____

20. Jon doesn't know how lucky he is. _____

Name _____   Date _____

Compound Words

- A **compound** word is a word that is made up of two or more words.
- The meaning of compound words is related to the meaning of each individual word.
  - EXAMPLE: sail + boat = sailboat, meaning "a boat that uses sails to move through water"
- Compound words may be written as one word, as hyphenated words, or as separate words.
  - EXAMPLES: airport   air-condition   air force

 Combine the words from the box to make compound words. You may use words more than once.

sand	fall	paper	color	home	water	room	play
made	field	under	come	out	stand	mate	back

1. _____   7. _____
2. _____   8. _____
3. _____   9. _____
4. _____   10. _____
5. _____   11. _____
6. _____   12. _____

Answer the following questions.

13. The word <u>books</u> sometimes refers to "financial accounts."

    What is a <u>bookkeeper</u>? _____

14. A <u>fast</u> is "a period of time when a person eats little or nothing."

    What does <u>breakfast</u> actually mean? _____

15. <u>Ferry</u> means "to transport across a body of water."

    What is a <u>ferryboat</u>? _____

16. A <u>lord</u> is "a person who has great authority over something."

    What is a <u>landlord</u>? _____

17. A <u>toll</u> is "a charge for permission to pass over a bridge or along a highway."

    What is a <u>tollbooth</u>? _____

18. Since <u>out</u> means "outside of," what is an <u>outlaw</u>?

    _____

Language: Usage and Practice 8, SV 1419027859

Connotation/Denotation

> - The **denotation** of a word is its exact meaning as stated in a dictionary.
>   EXAMPLE: The denotation of <u>casual</u> is "not fancy or formal."
> - The **connotation** of a word is an added meaning that suggests something positive or negative.
>   EXAMPLES: **Negative:** <u>Sloppy</u> suggests "very messy." <u>Sloppy</u> has a negative connotation.
>   **Positive:** <u>Casual</u> suggests "informal or relaxed." <u>Casual</u> has a positive connotation.
> - Some words are neutral. They do not suggest either good or bad feelings.
>   EXAMPLES: calendar   toy   pencil

Write (–) if the word has a negative connotation. Write (+) if it has a positive connotation. Write (N) if the word is neutral.

1. _____ lazy
   _____ relaxed

2. _____ determined
   _____ stubborn

3. _____ drug
   _____ remedy

4. _____ clever
   _____ sneaky

5. _____ pretty
   _____ gorgeous

6. _____ grand
   _____ large

7. _____ old
   _____ antique

8. _____ curious
   _____ nosy

9. _____ make
   _____ create

10. _____ weird
    _____ unique

11. _____ criticize
    _____ evaluate

12. _____ snooty
    _____ refined

Rewrite the paragraph below. Replace the underlined words with words that do not have a negative connotation.

Jason <u>shoved</u> his way through the <u>mob</u> of people. He <u>swaggered</u> through the doorway and <u>slouched</u> against the wall. His clothes were quite <u>gaudy</u>. He <u>glared</u> at everyone with <u>hostile</u> eyes. Then he <u>snickered</u> and said in a <u>loud</u> tone, "I'm finally here."

_____

_____

_____

_____

_____

_____

_____

_____

Language: Usage and Practice 8, SV 1419027859

Idioms

> • An **idiom** is an expression that has a meaning different from the usual meanings of the individual words within it.
>   EXAMPLE: We're all in the same boat usually means "We're in a similar situation," not "We're all in a watercraft together."

 Read each sentence. Then write the letter of the corresponding idiom for the underlined word or words.

A. shaken up	**D.** beside herself	**G.** comes through	**J.** down in the dumps
B. fly off the handle	**E.** in a bind	**H.** in the doghouse	**K.** stands up for
C. on cloud nine	**F.** put up with	**I.** on the fence	

1. One day Julia will be <u>sad</u>. _____

2. The next day you may find her <u>unbelievably happy</u>. _____

3. But be careful when Julia is <u>very scared or confused</u>. _____

4. She's liable to <u>become suddenly angry</u>. _____

5. Julia always <u>defends</u> her views, no matter what. _____

6. She won't <u>allow</u> any argument. _____

7. One time when I insisted that she listen to my viewpoint, she was <u>really upset</u>. _____

8. I was <u>out of favor</u> for weeks. _____

9. On the other hand, when a friend of Julia's is <u>in a difficult situation</u>, she really <u>helps</u>. _____

10. Like a true friend, Julia is there when I am <u>unable to make a decision</u>. _____

 For the underlined idiom in each sentence below, write the usual meaning of the words that make up the idiom.

11. Kelly can't decide whether she wants to go, so our plans are still <u>up in the air</u>. _____

12. If I get the job, I'll be <u>walking on air</u>. _____

13. My friend's business is <u>on the skids</u>. _____

14. George's ideas are <u>off the wall</u>. _____

15. That's enough silliness. Let's <u>talk turkey</u>. _____

16. Victor was <u>in hot water</u> for not cleaning the garage. _____

17. The audience was <u>all ears</u> when you spoke. _____

18. The lost book <u>turned up</u> yesterday. _____

19. Carli and I <u>put our heads together</u> to solve the problem. _____

Unit 1 Test

Choose whether the underlined words in each sentence are synonyms, antonyms, homonyms, or homographs. Darken the circle by your choice.

1. After you <u>complete</u> the test, please <u>finish</u> your homework.

    Ⓐ synonyms   Ⓑ antonyms   Ⓒ homonyms   Ⓓ homographs

2. We almost <u>missed</u> the stop sign because of the <u>mist</u> in the air.

    Ⓐ synonyms   Ⓑ antonyms   Ⓒ homonyms   Ⓓ homographs

3. Is there a <u>solution</u> to every <u>problem</u>?

    Ⓐ synonyms   Ⓑ antonyms   Ⓒ homonyms   Ⓓ homographs

4. The lawyer who represented their <u>firm</u> took a very <u>firm</u> stand.

    Ⓐ synonyms   Ⓑ antonyms   Ⓒ homonyms   Ⓓ homographs

5. After his injury, he had to learn to <u>write</u> with his <u>right</u> hand.

    Ⓐ synonyms   Ⓑ antonyms   Ⓒ homonyms   Ⓓ homographs

6. She <u>stayed</u> for only a week, but he <u>remained</u> for the entire summer.

    Ⓐ synonyms   Ⓑ antonyms   Ⓒ homonyms   Ⓓ homographs

7. Their last disagreement was the <u>beginning</u> of the <u>end</u> of their friendship.

    Ⓐ synonyms   Ⓑ antonyms   Ⓒ homonyms   Ⓓ homographs

Add a prefix or suffix to the underlined word to make a new word that makes sense in the sentence. Darken the circle by your choice.

8. We made the <u>pay</u> on time.

    Ⓐ pre   Ⓒ ment
    Ⓑ un   Ⓓ able

9. Please <u>warn</u> me of any dangers.

    Ⓐ un   Ⓒ ful
    Ⓑ fore   Ⓓ im

10. Did Leo <u>wrap</u> his present?

    Ⓐ un   Ⓒ y
    Ⓑ fore   Ⓓ il

11. Carmen is full of <u>kind</u>.

    Ⓐ ful   Ⓒ ment
    Ⓑ less   Ⓓ ness

Darken the circle by the correct prefix or suffix for the meaning given.

12. without

    Ⓐ ful   Ⓒ ment
    Ⓑ less   Ⓓ ness

13. before

    Ⓐ fore   Ⓒ un
    Ⓑ less   Ⓓ ly

14. act or process of

    Ⓐ ful   Ⓒ ment
    Ⓑ im   Ⓓ tion

15. again

    Ⓐ pre   Ⓒ re
    Ⓑ ish   Ⓓ ment

Language: Usage and Practice 8, SV 1419027859

Unit 1 Test, p. 2

Choose whether each word has a prefix, a suffix, or is a compound word. Darken the circle by your choice.

16. tugboat   Ⓐ prefix   Ⓑ suffix   Ⓒ compound word
17. incomplete   Ⓐ prefix   Ⓑ suffix   Ⓒ compound word
18. comfortable   Ⓐ prefix   Ⓑ suffix   Ⓒ compound word
19. weekend   Ⓐ prefix   Ⓑ suffix   Ⓒ compound word
20. reinstall   Ⓐ prefix   Ⓑ suffix   Ⓒ compound word
21. forefather   Ⓐ prefix   Ⓑ suffix   Ⓒ compound word
22. graceful   Ⓐ prefix   Ⓑ suffix   Ⓒ compound word
23. blackbird   Ⓐ prefix   Ⓑ suffix   Ⓒ compound word

Darken the circle by the compound word that matches the meaning.

24. excluded from a group   Ⓐ outboard   Ⓑ outcast   Ⓒ outback
25. a fixed marker that indicates a boundary line   Ⓐ landmass   Ⓑ landmark   Ⓒ landlocked
26. a ruthless person   Ⓐ cutup   Ⓑ cutthroat   Ⓒ cutout

Darken the circle by the correct contraction for each pair of underlined words.

27. <u>should not</u>
Ⓐ shouldn't   Ⓒ should't
Ⓑ should'nt   Ⓓ shoud'nt

28. <u>they are</u>
Ⓐ they'r   Ⓒ theyr'e
Ⓑ their'   Ⓓ they're

29. <u>what is</u>
Ⓐ wha's   Ⓒ whats'
Ⓑ what's   Ⓓ what'

30. <u>will not</u>
Ⓐ willn't   Ⓒ won't
Ⓑ wont'   Ⓓ will'nt

Choose whether each underlined word has a positive connotation (+), a negative connotation (–), or is neutral (N). Darken the circle by your choice.

31. The party was <u>dull</u>.   Ⓐ (+)   Ⓑ (–)   Ⓒ (N)
32. That's a <u>fascinating</u> book.   Ⓐ (+)   Ⓑ (–)   Ⓒ (N)
33. Can you <u>join</u> us?   Ⓐ (+)   Ⓑ (–)   Ⓒ (N)
34. Carla is very <u>gracious</u>.   Ⓐ (+)   Ⓑ (–)   Ⓒ (N)
35. Did you hear that <u>gossip</u>?   Ⓐ (+)   Ⓑ (–)   Ⓒ (N)
36. We painted the <u>garage</u>.   Ⓐ (+)   Ⓑ (–)   Ⓒ (N)

Name _____ Date _____

Recognizing Sentences

> • A **sentence** is a group of words that expresses a complete thought.
>   EXAMPLE: He has not worked since he injured his leg.

✳ **Some of the following groups of words are sentences, and some are not. Write S before each group that is a sentence. Punctuate each sentence with a period.**

_____ 1. In planning our work schedule _____

_____ 2. December is the last month of the year _____

_____ 3. Last year when it snowed for eight days _____

_____ 4. Another way to improve the quality of your voice _____

_____ 5. The largest city in Illinois is Chicago _____

_____ 6. There is no way to know what will happen _____

_____ 7. Enter the house very quietly _____

_____ 8. On one of our hikes in the park _____

_____ 9. Houston is the largest gulf port _____

_____ 10. An outstanding quarterback with the ability to throw long passes _____

_____ 11. Paul Revere was a silversmith _____

_____ 12. Check all your sentences carefully _____

_____ 13. High on a wooded hill, the cabin _____

_____ 14. The cats had a wonderful time running among the bushes _____

_____ 15. After wading a long distance in the stream _____

_____ 16. As the hour approached for the program _____

_____ 17. Kathleen has been learning to become a mechanic _____

_____ 18. Don't throw those papers away _____

_____ 19. California is the third largest state in the United States _____

_____ 20. There are many mountain streams in the Ozarks _____

_____ 21. Before they reached the edge of the cliff _____

_____ 22. Many notable Americans are buried in the National Cathedral _____

_____ 23. In the early morning, the wind became cold _____

_____ 24. The silvery airplane _____

_____ 25. From the spaceship onto the carrier _____

_____ 26. Here comes the delivery truck _____

_____ 27. W. C. Handy was a famous blues musician _____

_____ 28. While on vacation in Florida _____

_____ 29. Breathless with excitement and joy _____

_____ 30. Laurie and I picked apples this morning _____

Types of Sentences

> • A **declarative sentence** makes a statement. It is followed by a period (.).
>   EXAMPLE: Insects have six legs.
> • An **interrogative sentence** asks a question. It is followed by a question mark (?).
>   EXAMPLE: What are you eating?
> • An **imperative sentence** expresses a command or request. It is followed by a period.
>   EXAMPLE: Open the window.
> • An **exclamatory sentence** expresses strong emotion. It can also express a command or request that is made with great excitement. It is followed by an exclamation point (!).
>   EXAMPLES: The grass is on fire! Hurry over here!

 Write **D** for declarative, **IN** for interrogative, **IM** for imperative, or **E** for exclamatory before each sentence. Put the correct punctuation at the end of each sentence.

_____   1. What do you consider a fair price ____

_____   2. How many people signed a contract ____

_____   3. Do not leave objects lying on floors and stairways ____

_____   4. Mary Bethune became the first black woman to head a federal agency ____

_____   5. What a cold day it is ____

_____   6. Ryan, where have you been ____

_____   7. Return those books when you finish them ____

_____   8. I bought this scarf in Mexico ____

_____   9. Look at that gorgeous sunset ____

_____   10. Copy each problem accurately ____

_____   11. Books are storehouses of knowledge ____

_____   12. My pet snake is loose ____

_____   13. How do forests help prevent floods ____

_____   14. Where did we get the word September ____

_____   15. Listen attentively ____

_____   16. Rice is the most widely eaten food in the world ____

_____   17. Don't lose the book ____

_____   18. Paul's cousins from South Dakota will arrive Saturday ____

_____   19. Did you buy more cereal ____

_____   20. We saw the new tiger exhibit at the zoo ____

_____   21. Put those books on that shelf ____

_____   22. Do you want to help me make bread ____

_____   23. We're out of flour ____

_____   24. Wait for me ____

_____   25. How old is that oak tree ____

Language: Usage and Practice 8, SV 1419027859

Complete Subjects and Predicates

> - Every sentence has two main parts, a **complete subject** and a **complete predicate.**
> - The complete subject includes all the words that tell who or what the sentence is about.
>   - EXAMPLE: **The southern section of our state** / has many forests.
> - The complete predicate includes all the words that state the action or condition of the subject.
>   - EXAMPLE: The southern section of our state / **has many forests.**

 Draw a line between the complete subject and the complete predicate in each sentence below.

1. An earthquake formed Reelfoot Lake in 1811.

2. The deepest places in the oceans are in the Mariana Trench in the Pacific.

3. The seasons are the four divisions of the year.

4. Many of the people waited instead of crowding into the bus.

5. The two mechanics have not yet fixed the car.

6. The first telegraph line was between Baltimore, Maryland, and Washington, D.C.

7. The territory of Iowa was formed from a part of the Louisiana Purchase.

8. The origin of the wheat plant is very obscure.

9. The television tube was a product of many years of experimentation.

10. The shortest day of the year is in December.

11. Workers discussed timely topics at the meeting.

12. Fossils show that ferns 100 feet high once grew in Kansas.

13. Great deposits of bauxite, from which aluminum is extracted, exist in Arkansas.

14. The Shoshone live in Wyoming, Idaho, and Nevada.

15. The citizens of Georgia built Fort Pulaski over one hundred years ago.

16. Who originated Father's Day?

17. Many people watched the airliner take off.

18. Mexican silver mines were worked before the Spanish conquest.

19. A steamboat was used on the Mississippi River for the first time in 1811.

20. Who brought in the mail?

21. Benjamin Franklin was once an apprentice to his brother.

22. All of the guests enjoyed the picnic.

23. Annapolis Academy was founded in 1845.

24. The three cities that we visited were New York, Montreal, and Calgary.

25. Banff National Park is one of the most popular parks in Canada.

26. Many towns in the United States are built around squares.

Language: Usage and Practice 8, SV 1419027859

Simple Subjects and Predicates

> • The **simple subject** of a sentence is the main word in the complete subject.
> • The simple subject is a noun or a pronoun. Sometimes the simple subject is also the complete subject.
>   EXAMPLES:
>   The southern **section** of our state / has many forests.
>   **Forests** / are beautiful.
> • The **simple predicate** of a sentence is a verb within the complete predicate.
> • The verb may be made up of one word or more than one word.
>   EXAMPLES:
>   Dogs / **have** good hearing.
>   Maria / **is going.**

 Draw a line between the complete subject and the complete predicate in each sentence below. Then underline the simple subject once and the simple predicate twice.

1. The different <u>meanings</u> for that word / <u>cover</u> half of a dictionary page.
2. A valuable oil is made from peanuts.
3. A beautiful highway winds through the Catskill Mountains.
4. The woman in the black dress studied the painting for over an hour.
5. The meadowlark builds its nest on the ground.
6. The making of ice cream can be much fun.
7. Many stories have been written about the old Spanish Main, the northern coast of South America.
8. His answer to the question was incorrect.
9. Every sentence should begin with a capital letter.
10. The rotation of Earth on its axis causes day and night.
11. In Norway, a narrow inlet of the sea between cliffs is called a fjord.
12. The Dutch cultivated large fields of tulips and hyacinths.
13. The two treasury mints in the United States are located in Philadelphia and Denver.
14. Benjamin Franklin's *Poor Richard's Almanac* is filled with wise sayings.
15. The warm climate of Jamaica attracts many winter tourists.
16. That movie has been shown on television many times.
17. Acres of wheat rippled in the breeze.
18. That mechanic completed the job in record time.
19. The people in that picture were boarding a plane for London.
20. One can find rocks of fantastic shapes in the Garden of the Gods, near Colorado Springs, Colorado.
21. The city of Albuquerque is five thousand feet above sea level.
22. The apple trees have fragrant blossoms.
23. Sequoias, the world's tallest trees, are found in California.
24. John Banister was an early botanist.
25. The tall pine trees hide our tiny cabin.
26. The woman filled the vase with colorful flowers.

Language: Usage and Practice 8, SV 1419027859

Position of Subjects

- When the subject of a sentence comes before the verb, the sentence is in **natural order.**
  EXAMPLE: Henry <u>went</u> to the park.
- When the verb or part of the verb comes before the subject, the sentence is in **inverted order.**
  EXAMPLES:
  Here <u>are</u> the calculators.
  Down <u>came</u> the rain.
- Many questions are in inverted order.
  EXAMPLE: Where <u>is</u> the restaurant?
- Sometimes the subject of a sentence is not expressed, as in a command or request. The understood subject is <u>you.</u>
  EXAMPLES:
  <u>Call</u> about the job now.
  (You) <u>call</u> about the job now.

 Rewrite each inverted sentence in natural order. Underline the simple subject once and the simple predicate twice. Add <u>you</u> as the subject to commands or requests.

1. When is the movie playing?

_____

2. Never will I forget my first train trip.

_____

3. Here is the picture I want to buy.

_____

4. Seldom has he been ill.

_____

5. Out went the lights.

_____

6. There were bookcases on all sides of the room.

_____

7. Take the roast from the oven.

_____

8. Around the sharp curve swerved the speeding car.

_____

9. Get out of the swimming pool.

_____

10. Study for the spelling test.

_____

11. There are two children in the pool.

_____

Language: Usage and Practice 8, SV 1419027859

Compound Subjects and Predicates

> • A **compound subject** is made up of two or more simple subjects.
>   EXAMPLE: **Matt** and **Jan** / are great swimmers.
> • A **compound predicate** is made up of two or more simple predicates.
>   EXAMPLE: The dog / **ran** and **barked** with joy.

 Draw a line between the complete subject and the complete predicate in each sentence. Underline the compound subject once or the compound predicate twice in each sentence.

1. Lewis and Clark blazed a trail across the North American continent.

2. The rose and the jasmine are important flowers for perfume manufacturing.

3. Kelly and Amy went with us.

4. Chris swept the floor, dusted the furniture, and washed the windows.

5. Empires flourish and decay.

6. The level of the lake rises and falls several times each year.

7. Juanita and her brother are excellent skaters.

8. Dwight D. Eisenhower and Douglas MacArthur were famous American generals.

9. He turned slowly and then answered my question.

10. Museums, libraries, and art galleries are found in many cities.

11. The computers, the desks, and the chairs are all new.

12. The plants grew tall and flowered.

13. Aseret and Teresa worked hard.

14. He ran and slid into third base.

15. The salesclerk added up the numbers and wrote down the total.

16. Reading and baking are her favorite pastimes.

17. Mary drank iced tea and ate a sandwich.

18. Cars and trucks sped past.

19. Red and blue are his favorite colors.

 Write two sentences containing compound subjects.

20. _____

21. _____

 Write two sentences containing compound predicates.

22. _____

23. _____

Language: Usage and Practice 8, SV 1419027859

Combining Sentences

- Two sentences in which the subjects are different and the predicates are the same can be combined into one sentence.
- The two subjects are joined by <u>and</u>.
  - EXAMPLE:
    The sun is part of our solar system. **The nine planets** are part of our solar system.
    The sun and nine planets are part of our solar system.
- Two sentences in which the subjects are the same and the predicates are different can be combined into one sentence.
- The two predicates may be joined by <u>or</u>, <u>and</u>, or <u>but</u>.
  - EXAMPLE:
    The planets **are the largest bodies moving around the sun.** The planets **have a total of 34 moons.**
    The planets **are the largest bodies moving around the sun and have a total of 34 moons.**

 Combine each pair of sentences below. Underline the compound subject or the compound predicate in each sentence that you write.

1. The nine planets in our solar system vary in size. The nine planets in our solar system are at different distances from the sun.

_____

_____

2. Mercury does not have any moons. Venus does not have any moons.

_____

3. Venus is similar in some ways to Earth. Venus is much hotter than Earth.

_____

4. Pluto is the farthest planet from the sun. Pluto takes 248 years to revolve around the sun.

_____

5. Planets revolve around the sun in regular paths. Planets also rotate and spin like tops.

_____

_____

6. Mercury revolves around the sun in less than a year. Venus revolves around the sun in less than a year.

_____

_____

7. The solar system may have been formed in a collision between the sun and another star. The solar system may have come from a cloud of gas.

_____

_____

Language: Usage and Practice 8, SV 1419027859

Name _____ Date _____

Direct Objects

> - The **direct object** tells who or what receives the action of the verb.
> - The direct object is a noun or pronoun that follows an action verb.
>
> $$\text{EXAMPLE: } \quad \overset{DO}{\text{Those countries export \textbf{coffee}.}}$$

 Underline the verb in each sentence. Then write <u>DO</u> above each direct object.

1. Juanita's good driving prevented an accident.

2. Every person should have an appreciation of music.

3. Gene, pass the potatoes, please.

4. Do not waste your time on this project.

5. Jim, did you keep those coupons?

6. Geraldo collects foreign stamps.

7. Eli Whitney invented the cotton gin.

8. Answer my question.

9. We are picking trophies for our bowling league.

10. Who invented the steamboat?

11. I am reading Hemingway's *The Old Man and the Sea.*

12. The North Star guides sailors.

13. The Phoenicians gave the alphabet to civilization.

14. Every person should study world history.

15. Who made this cake?

16. Can you find a direct object in this sentence?

17. Who wrote the story of Johnny Tremain?

18. We bought several curios for our friends.

19. Tamara read the minutes of our last club meeting.

20. Did you ever make a time budget of your own?

21. Mountains have often affected the history of a nation.

22. Emma and Joe baked a pie.

Indirect Objects

Direct Objects

> - The **indirect object** is the noun or pronoun that tells to whom or for whom an action is done.
> - In order to have an indirect object, a sentence must have a direct object.
> - The indirect object is usually placed between the action verb and the direct object.
>
>   IO   DO

 Underline the verb in each sentence. Then write DO above the direct object and IO above the indirect object.

1. The pitcher threw Dave a fastball.

2. We gave the usher our tickets.

3. The doctor handed Chris the prescription.

4. Mr. Lewis sold us a set of encyclopedias.

5. Have you written Andrea a note about the time of our arrival?

6. The supervisor paid the employee a high salary.

7. Experience should teach us wisdom.

8. Who sent Amy that long letter?

9. Maria, show us that magic trick.

10. I gave the cashier the money for our tickets.

11. Many years ago, a clever writer gave us the story of Robinson Crusoe.

12. A guide always shows visitors the interesting things in this museum.

13. Working crossword puzzles gives many people hours of enjoyment.

14. Carlos, give the group a lecture on saving money.

15. The study of space travel has brought us many new inventions.

16. Dale, please take Sandra these books.

17. Mrs. Yonge gave Joanna several plants.

18. Please give me a drink of water.

19. Who gave the United States flag the name Old Glory?

20. Will you give me those instructions again?

Language: Usage and Practice 8, SV 1419027859

Name _____ Date _____

Independent and Subordinate Clauses

> - A **clause** is a group of words that contains a subject and a predicate.
> - There are two kinds of clauses: independent clauses and subordinate clauses.
> - An **independent clause** can stand alone as a sentence because it expresses a complete thought.
>   - EXAMPLE: **He recovered the watch** that he had lost.

 Underline the independent clause in each sentence below.

1. We arrived late because we couldn't find the theater.
2. The play started before we found our seats.
3. We got one of the special programs that were being sold.
4. When the play was over, the audience applauded.
5. After we saw the show, we went for a walk.
6. Although the night was cool, the walk was enjoyable.
7. While we were walking, I noticed the moon.
8. Since it was a full moon, it was shining brightly.
9. We walked along the lake until it became very late.
10. By the time I got home, it was almost midnight.

> - A **subordinate clause** has a subject and predicate but cannot stand alone as a sentence because it does not express a complete thought.
> - A subordinate clause must be combined with an independent clause to make a sentence.
>   - EXAMPLE: We started **when the sun rose.**

 Underline the subordinate clause in each sentence below.

11. Japan is a country where some trains travel at very fast speeds.
12. The airplane that we saw can land in only a few airports in this country.
13. Henry Hudson discovered the river that bears his name.
14. When you respect others, you win respect for yourself.
15. Diego found the new job that was perfect for him.
16. Colleen is the one who was elected without a run-off.
17. The coin that I purchased is an old French crown.
18. When I awoke, it was broad daylight.
19. Those who would control others must first control themselves.
20. The camel is the only pack animal that can stand the test of the Sahara.

Name _____ Date _____

Adjective and Adverb Clauses

- An **adjective clause** is a subordinate clause that modifies a noun or a pronoun.
- It answers the adjective question <u>Which one?</u> or <u>What kind?</u>
- It usually modifies the word directly preceding it.
- Most adjective clauses begin with a **relative pronoun.** A relative pronoun relates an adjective clause to the noun or pronoun that the clause modifies.
- <u>Who</u>, <u>whom</u>, <u>whose</u>, <u>which</u>, and <u>that</u> are relative pronouns.
  EXAMPLE: Always do the work **that is assigned to you.**
                            adjective clause

- An **adverb clause** is a subordinate clause that modifies a verb, an adjective, or another adverb.
- It answers the adverb question <u>How?</u>, <u>Under what condition?</u>, or <u>Why?</u>
- Words that introduce adverb clauses are called **subordinating conjunctions.**
- The many subordinating conjunctions include such words as <u>when</u>, <u>after</u>, <u>before</u>, <u>since</u>, <u>although</u>, and <u>because</u>.
  EXAMPLE: We left **when the storm clouds gathered.**
                            adverb clause

✳ **Underline the subordinate clause. Then write <u>adjective</u> or <u>adverb</u> on the line to tell what kind of clause it is.**

_____ **1.** John Paul Jones was a hero whose bravery won many victories.

_____ **2.** The person who reads the most books will get a prize.

_____ **3.** He overslept because he hadn't set the alarm.

_____ **4.** Give a rousing cheer when our team comes off the field.

_____ **5.** The parrot repeats many things that he hears.

_____ **6.** The picnic that we planned was canceled.

✳ **Add a subordinate clause beginning with the word in parentheses to each independent clause below.**

7. The package was gone (when) _____

_____

8. A depot is a place (where) _____

_____

9. Brad and I cannot go now (because) _____

_____

10. Tell me the name of the person (who) _____

_____

Name _____   Date _____

Compound and Complex Sentences

> - A **compound sentence** consists of two or more independent clauses.
> - Each independent clause in a compound sentence can stand alone as a separate sentence.
> - The independent clauses are usually joined by <u>and</u>, <u>but</u>, <u>so</u>, <u>or</u>, <u>for</u>, or <u>yet</u> and a comma.
>   EXAMPLE: I like to dance, but Lyle likes to sing.
> - Sometimes a **semicolon (;)** is used to join the independent clauses in a compound sentence.
>   EXAMPLE: I like to dance; Lyle likes to sing.
> - A **complex sentence** consists of one independent clause and one or more subordinate clauses.
>   EXAMPLE: **When the fire alarm went off**, everyone left the building.
>   subordinate clause

✳ **Write <u>CP</u> before each compound sentence. Write <u>CX</u> before each complex sentence.**

_____ 1. Our team didn't always win, but we always tried to be good sports.

_____ 2. You may stay, but I am going home.

_____ 3. The rangers who serve in Yellowstone Park know every inch of the ground.

_____ 4. That statement may be correct, but it isn't very polite.

_____ 5. We will meet whenever we can.

_____ 6. The pass was thrown perfectly, but Carlos was too well guarded to catch it.

_____ 7. The toga was worn by ancient Roman youths when they reached the age of twelve.

_____ 8. That song, which is often heard on the radio, was written years ago.

_____ 9. They cannot come for dinner, but they will be here later.

_____ 10. My brother likes dogs, but I prefer cats.

_____ 11. The engine is the heart of the submarine, and the periscope is the eye.

_____ 12. I will call you when it arrives.

_____ 13. Those people who camped here were messy.

_____ 14. Edison was only thirty years old when he invented the talking machine.

_____ 15. She crept silently, for she was afraid.

_____ 16. Move the table, but be careful with it.

_____ 17. Bolivia is the only South American country that does not have a port.

_____ 18. How many stars were in the flag that Key saw "by the dawn's early light"?

_____ 19. The octopus gets its name from two Greek words that mean <u>eight</u> and <u>feet</u>.

_____ 20. You may place the order, but we cannot guarantee shipment.

_____ 21. After the sun set, we built a campfire.

_____ 22. We made hamburgers for dinner, and then we toasted marshmallows.

_____ 23. Some people sang songs; others played games.

_____ 24. When it started to rain, everyone took shelter in the tents.

Language: Usage and Practice 8, SV 1419027859

Compound and Complex Sentences, p. 2

 Put brackets [ ] around the independent clauses in each compound sentence below. Then underline the simple subject once and the simple predicate twice in each clause.

25. The streets are filled with cars, but the sidewalks are empty.

26. Those apples are too sour to eat, but those pears are perfect.

27. She studies hard, but she saves some time to enjoy herself.

28. They lost track of time, so they were late.

29. Eric had not studied, so he failed the test.

30. Yesterday it rained all day, but today the sun is shining.

31. I set the alarm to get up early, but I couldn't get up.

32. They may sing and dance until dawn, but they will be exhausted.

33. My friend moved to Texas, and I will miss her.

34. They arrived at the theater early, but there was still a long line.

35. Lisa took her dog to the veterinarian, but his office was closed.

36. The black cat leaped, but fortunately it didn't catch the bird.

37. I found a baseball in the bushes, and I gave it to my brother.

38. We loaded the cart with groceries, and we went to the checkout.

39. The stadium was showered with lights, but the stands were empty.

40. The small child whimpered, and her mother hugged her.

41. The dark clouds rolled in, and then it began to rain.

 In each complex sentence below, underline the subordinate clause.

42. The hummingbird is the only bird that can fly backward.

43. The cat that is sitting in the window is mine.

44. The car that is parked outside is new.

45. Brett, who is a football star, is class president.

46. Bonnie, who is an artist, is also studying computer science.

47. Jason likes food that is cooked in the microwave.

48. The composer who wrote the music comes from Germany.

49. We missed seeing him because we were late.

50. When Jake arrives, we will tell him what happened.

51. She walked slowly because she had hurt her leg.

52. When she walked to the podium, everyone applauded.

53. If animals could talk, they might have a lot to tell.

54. Many roads that were built in our city are no longer traveled.

55. My address book, which is bright red, is gone.

56. Ann, who is from Georgia, just started working here today.

57. The crowd cheered when the player came to bat.

58. When he hit the ball, everyone cheered.

Correcting Run-on Sentences

- Two or more independent clauses that are run together without the correct punctuation are called a **run-on sentence.**
    EXAMPLE: Your brain is an amazing organ you could not read without it.
- One way to correct a run-on sentence is to separate it into two sentences.
    EXAMPLE: Your brain is an amazing organ. You could not read without it.
- Another way to correct a run-on sentence is to make it into a compound sentence.
    EXAMPLE: Your brain is an amazing organ, and you could not read without it.
- Another way to correct a run-on sentence is to use a semicolon.
    EXAMPLE: Your brain is an amazing organ; you could not read without it.

 Correct each run-on sentence below by writing it as two sentences or as a compound sentence.

1. The brain is surrounded by three membranes the skull encloses the brain and these three membranes.

    _____

    _____

2. The brain reaches its full size by the time a person is twenty at that time, it weighs about three pounds.

    _____

    _____

3. The brain helps a person see, hear, touch, smell, and taste it also makes it possible for one to remember and forget, talk and write, and feel emotions.

    _____

    _____

4. The brain has three main parts these parts are the cerebrum, the cerebellum, and the brain stem.

    _____

    _____

5. A computer is like a human brain however, a computer would have to be the size of a skyscraper to perform all of the functions of the human brain.

    _____

    _____

    _____

Language: Usage and Practice 8, SV 1419027859

Name _____ Date _____

Expanding Sentences

- Sentences can be **expanded** by adding details to make them clearer and more interesting.
  EXAMPLE:
  The dog ran.
  The **big black** dog ran **barking into the street.**
- Details added to sentences may answer these questions: When? Where? How? How often? To what degree? What kind? Which? How many?

 Expand each sentence below by adding details to answer the questions shown in parentheses. Write the expanded sentence on the line.

1. The crew was ready for liftoff. (Which? When?)

_____

2. The shuttle was launched. (What kind? Where?)

_____

3. The engines roared. (How many? To what degree?)

_____

4. The spacecraft shot up. (How? Where?)

_____

5. The astronauts studied the control panels. (How many? Where?)

_____

 Decide how each of the following sentences can be expanded. Write your expanded sentence on the line.

6. The singer ran onto the stage.

_____

7. The fans leaped up and cheered.

_____

8. She began to sing.

_____

9. She strummed the guitar.

_____

10. The loudspeakers blared.

_____

11. The fans began dancing.

_____

Language: Usage and Practice 8, SV 1419027859

Unit 2 Test

Darken the circle by the correct sentence type.

1. When will you be back?
- Ⓐ declarative
- Ⓑ interrogative
- Ⓒ imperative
- Ⓓ exclamatory

2. What a wonderful surprise!
- Ⓐ declarative
- Ⓑ interrogative
- Ⓒ imperative
- Ⓓ exclamatory

3. Please leave me alone.
- Ⓐ declarative
- Ⓑ interrogative
- Ⓒ imperative
- Ⓓ exclamatory

4. I wish this rain would stop.
- Ⓐ declarative
- Ⓑ interrogative
- Ⓒ imperative
- Ⓓ exclamatory

Darken the circle by the sentence in which the complete subject is underlined.

5.
- Ⓐ The agency designed a beautiful brochure.
- Ⓑ Tiffany and Mary Ellen are twins.
- Ⓒ Our cars are the same make and model.
- Ⓓ The end of the movie came all too soon.

Darken the circle by the sentence in which the complete predicate is underlined.

6.
- Ⓐ We spent the day skiing and skating.
- Ⓑ Please give me your hand.
- Ⓒ Go ask Erika for the key.
- Ⓓ First, deliver the letter.

Darken the circle by the sentence in which the simple subject is underlined.

7.
- Ⓐ Those are my brother's records.
- Ⓑ Your turn is next.
- Ⓒ There are many varieties of fish.
- Ⓓ Our house is made of brick.

Darken the circle by the sentence in which the simple predicate is underlined.

8.
- Ⓐ Would you like to go with us?
- Ⓑ I am not going to the party.
- Ⓒ Mr. Wong owns a shoe store.
- Ⓓ When did Trish say good-bye?

Darken the circle by the sentence in which the compound subject is underlined.

9.
- Ⓐ Paul asked his friend to leave.
- Ⓑ Lily and Dana like to compete.
- Ⓒ The dog growled and barked.
- Ⓓ Oatmeal and fruit make a good breakfast.

Darken the circle by the sentence in which the compound predicate is underlined.

10.
- Ⓐ Chad cheered and clapped.
- Ⓑ They planted and watered the seeds.
- Ⓒ Sallee and Dave agreed to the sale.
- Ⓓ Why did he grumble and moan?

Darken the circle by the term that correctly identifies the underlined word.

11. We swam for hours each day at camp.
 Ⓐ indirect object Ⓑ direct object Ⓒ neither

12. Would you please give me your new phone number?
 Ⓐ indirect object Ⓑ direct object Ⓒ neither

13. I made my sister a swing from some rope and a board.
 Ⓐ indirect object Ⓑ direct object Ⓒ neither

14. Last summer I taught children sign language.
 Ⓐ indirect object Ⓑ direct object Ⓒ neither

15. Did Diane write you a letter while she was away?
 Ⓐ indirect object Ⓑ direct object Ⓒ neither

Unit 2 Test, p. 2

Darken the circle by the term that correctly identifies the underlined group of words.

16. <u>Although I like to fish</u>, I don't care for baiting the hook.   Ⓐ adjective clause   Ⓑ adverb clause

17. The eagle <u>that soared over our heads</u> was very majestic.   Ⓐ adjective clause   Ⓑ adverb clause

18. We saw several deer <u>after we got far enough into the woods</u>.   Ⓐ adjective clause   Ⓑ adverb clause

19. Dimitri will take our picture <u>when he arrives</u>.   Ⓐ adjective clause   Ⓑ adverb clause

20. She started back home <u>because it was getting late</u>.   Ⓐ adjective clause   Ⓑ adverb clause

21. We left <u>before the rain began</u>.   Ⓐ adjective clause   Ⓑ adverb clause

22. We studied all of the paintings <u>that were in the exhibit</u>.   Ⓐ adjective clause   Ⓑ adverb clause

Darken the circle by the term that correctly identifies the group of words.

23. Under the porch ran the dog.
   Ⓐ compound sentence   Ⓑ complex sentence   Ⓒ sentence in inverted order

24. Did you see the geese this morning?
   Ⓐ compound sentence   Ⓑ complex sentence   Ⓒ sentence in inverted order

25. I would like to meet Kate, but she left for Canada today.
   Ⓐ compound sentence   Ⓑ complex sentence   Ⓒ sentence in inverted order

26. Eduardo is picking up litter in the alley, and he will be finished soon.
   Ⓐ compound sentence   Ⓑ complex sentence   Ⓒ sentence in inverted order

27. Over the steep hill came the speeding truck.
   Ⓐ compound sentence   Ⓑ complex sentence   Ⓒ sentence in inverted order

28. I can't wait; summer vacation starts in May.
   Ⓐ compound sentence   Ⓑ complex sentence   Ⓒ sentence in inverted order

29. Samuel will come to get you when he is ready.
   Ⓐ compound sentence   Ⓑ complex sentence   Ⓒ sentence in inverted order

30. They are the ones who started this project.
   Ⓐ compound sentence   Ⓑ complex sentence   Ⓒ sentence in inverted order

Darken the circle by the sentence that is a run-on sentence.

31. Ⓐ Have you ever seen the Leaning Tower of Pisa in Pisa, Italy?

   Ⓑ It's considered one of seven wonders of the world, it leans very far to one side.

   Ⓒ After three of its stories were built, the ground beneath the tower began to sink.

   Ⓓ Many say that Galileo conducted his experiments from this tower; others disagree.

32. Ⓐ The city council will vote today on building a new office, we hope they don't.

   Ⓑ Last year they decided they needed more space, but the public didn't approve.

   Ⓒ It almost seems as if they don't care what we think, doesn't it?

   Ⓓ The solution may be to vote them all out of office during the next election.

33. Ⓐ Justin and Sabrina decided to have a dinner party.

   Ⓑ They made a list of everything they would need.

   Ⓒ They went to the grocery store, they bought everything on the list.

   Ⓓ Everyone who went had a great time.

Language: Usage and Practice 8, SV 1419027859

Name _____   Date _____

Common and Proper Nouns

> • There are two main classes of **nouns**: common nouns and proper nouns.
> • A **common noun** names any one of a class of objects.
>   EXAMPLES: woman, city, tree
> • A **proper noun** names a particular person, place, or thing. It begins with a capital letter.
>   EXAMPLES: Ms. Patel, Chicago, Empire State Building

 Underline each noun. Then write C or P above it to show whether it is a common or proper noun.

      P   C

1. Maria is my sister.

2. Honolulu is the chief city and capital of Hawaii.

3. Rainbow Natural Bridge is hidden away in the wild mountainous part of southern Utah.

4. The Declaration of Independence is often called the birth certificate of the United States.

5. Abraham Lincoln, Edgar Allan Poe, and Frederic Chopin were born in the same year.

 Write a proper noun suggested by each common noun.

6. country _____   13. day _____

7. book _____   14. car _____

8. governor _____   15. lake _____

9. state _____   16. singer _____

10. athlete _____   17. holiday _____

11. school _____   18. newspaper _____

12. actor _____   19. river _____

 Write a sentence using each proper noun and the common noun for its class.

20. Mexico ____ Mexico is another country in North America. ____

21. December _____

22. Alaska _____

23. Thanksgiving Day _____

24. Abraham Lincoln _____

25. Tuesday _____

Unit 3: Grammar and Usage
Language: Usage and Practice 8, SV 1419027859

Concrete, Abstract, and Collective Nouns

- A **concrete noun** names things you can see and touch.
  EXAMPLES: apple, dog, fork, book, computer
- An **abstract noun** names an idea, quality, action, or feeling.
  EXAMPLES: bravery, wickedness, goodness
- A **collective noun** names a group of persons or things.
  EXAMPLES: crowd, congress, public, United States

Write concrete, collective, or abstract on the line to classify each common noun.

_____ 1. humor

_____ 2. kindness

_____ 3. army

_____ 4. danger

_____ 5. committee

_____ 6. towel

_____ 7. jury

_____ 8. audience

_____ 9. bird

_____ 10. orchestra

_____ 11. fear

_____ 12. family

_____ 13. happiness

_____ 14. truck

_____ 15. team

_____ 16. honesty

_____ 17. bracelet

_____ 18. society

_____ 19. album

_____ 20. courage

_____ 21. faculty

_____ 22. club

_____ 23. photograph

_____ 24. poverty

_____ 25. class

_____ 26. swarm

_____ 27. table

_____ 28. goodness

_____ 29. flock

_____ 30. radio

_____ 31. mob

_____ 32. patience

_____ 33. herd

_____ 34. banana

_____ 35. staff

_____ 36. mercy

_____ 37. calculator

_____ 38. coyote

_____ 39. generosity

_____ 40. scissors

_____ 41. sorrow

_____ 42. independence

Name _____ Date _____

Singular and Plural Nouns

The following chart shows how to change **singular nouns** into **plural nouns**.

Noun	Plural Form	Examples
Most nouns	Add <u>s</u>	ship, ships nose, noses
Nouns ending in a consonant and <u>y</u>	Change the <u>y</u> to <u>i</u> and add <u>es</u>	sky, skies navy, navies
Nouns ending in <u>o</u>	Add <u>s</u> or <u>es</u>	hero, heroes piano, pianos
Most nouns ending in <u>f</u> or <u>fe</u>	Change the <u>f</u> or <u>fe</u> to <u>ves</u>	half, halves
Most nouns ending in <u>ch</u>, <u>sh</u>, <u>s</u>, or <u>x</u>	Add <u>es</u>	bench, benches bush, bushes tax, taxes
Many two-word or three-word compound nouns	Add <u>s</u> to the principal word	son-in-law, sons-in-law
Nouns with the same form in the singular and plural	No change	sheep
Nouns with no singular form	No change	scissors
Nouns with irregular plurals	Change the entire word	foot, feet child, children
Figures, symbols, signs, letters, and words considered as words	Add an apostrophe and <u>s</u>	m, m's 5, 5's and, and's

 Write the plural for each singular noun.

1. county _____

2. pony _____

3. tomato _____

4. banjo _____

5. match _____

6. window _____

7. century _____

8. trench _____

9. bookcase _____

10. video _____

11. radio _____

12. farm _____

13. fly _____

14. hero _____

15. dress _____

16. boot _____

17. desk _____

18. daisy _____

Language: Usage and Practice 8, SV 1419027859

Singular and Plural Nouns, p. 2

 Write the singular form of each word below.

19. mouthfuls _____

20. proofs _____

21. 6's _____

22. calves _____

23. knives _____

24. Joneses _____

25. children _____

26. geese _____

27. wolves _____

28. roofs _____

29. gentlemen _____

30. editors-in-chief _____

31. +'s _____

32. cupfuls _____

33. trout _____

34. mice _____

 Write the plural form of the word in parentheses to complete each sentence. You may use a dictionary to check spellings.

35. (box)   Please store these _____ in the garage.

36. (city)   Can you name the four largest _____ in your state?

37. (deer)   The photographers brought back photos of three _____.

38. (flash)   The vivid _____ of lightning frightened everyone.

39. (coach)   That football team employs five _____.

40. (church)   Our small town has several beautiful _____

41. (potato)   Hot _____ were used as hand warmers in colonial days.

42. (e)   How many _____ are in the word Tennessee?

43. (O'Keefe)   The _____ are having a recital tonight.

44. (fish)   Where did you catch those _____?

45. (scarf)   Dale gave me three _____.

46. (n)   Cynthia, don't make your _____ look like u's.

47. (radio)   Kirk listens to two _____ so he can hear all the news.

48. (ox)   The _____ wore yokes around their necks.

49. (pilot)   Those _____ flew four round trips a day.

50. (90)   The teacher gave three _____ on the math test.

51. (woman)   A dozen _____ attended the conference.

52. (i)   Be sure you always dot your _____.

Language: Usage and Practice 8, SV 1419027859

Possessive Nouns

> • A **possessive noun** shows possession of the noun that follows.
>   EXAMPLES: Gerry's football, Donna's gloves
> • Form the possessive of most singular nouns by adding an apostrophe (') and <u>s</u>.
>   EXAMPLES: Jesse's pillow, Sandy's eyes
> • Form the possessive of most plural nouns ending in <u>s</u> by adding only an apostrophe.
>   EXAMPLES: birds' nest, lions' den
> • Form the possessive of plural nouns that do not end in <u>s</u> by adding an apostrophe and <u>s</u>.
>   EXAMPLES: men's shoes

 Underline the possessive nouns in each sentence.

1. Steve's glasses are on my desk.
2. Marcy is wearing her mother's gold bracelet.
3. My friends' club will meet at our house Monday night.
4. The woman's first statement caused us to change our minds.
5. We have formed a collector's club.
6. Rosa's brother found the child's lost puppy.
7. The Warrens' store was damaged by the recent storm.
8. What are the vice-president's duties?
9. When does the new mayor's term of office begin?
10. Leah, Tony's notebook is on your desk.
11. We went to the women's department.
12. The family's income was reduced.
13. Our day's work is done.
14. The lifeguards' heroism was rewarded.
15. Our team's defeat did not discourage us.
16. Has Joanna opened a children's store?
17. Juan's cooking is improving.
18. We borrowed Jim's hammer.
19. May I see Pedro's picture?
20. I'll meet you at the Chans' house.
21. Lucia visited Mark's college.
22. Frank's telephone call was about Lindsey's accident.
23. Mr. Clark stood at his neighbors' gate.
24. Is that the Masons' parking place?
25. Mexico's flag has an eagle holding a snake.

Appositives

> • An **appositive** is a noun or pronoun that identifies or explains the noun or pronoun it follows.
>   EXAMPLE: My German friend, **Gerhardt**, is coming to visit me next month.
> • An **appositive phrase** consists of an appositive and its modifiers.
>   EXAMPLE: Alta's school, **the junior high,** is sponsoring a dance.
> • Use commas to set off an appositive or an appositive phrase that is not essential to the meaning of the sentence.
>   EXAMPLE: Rico's nephew, **a twelve-year-old,** delivers newspapers.
> • Do not use commas if the appositive is essential to the meaning of the sentence.
>   EXAMPLE: The artist Picasso is my favorite.

 Underline each appositive word or phrase and circle the noun it identifies.

1. Jan Matzeliger, the inventor of the first shoemaking machine, was born in South America.

2. Niagara Falls, the natural wonder in New York, is not the tallest in the country.

3. Harvard, the oldest university in the United States, is in Massachusetts.

4. My brother Jim lives in Kansas.

5. Diane Feinstein, a mayor of San Francisco, was the first woman mayor of that city.

6. The Sears Tower, one of the tallest buildings in the world, is in Chicago.

7. Scott's cousin Liz sells antique cars.

8. Leontyne Price, the opera singer, was born in Mississippi.

9. The Pilgrim's ship, the *Mayflower*, had a stormy voyage.

10. Tom's dog Jasmine likes to swim.

11. Dr. Miller, our family physician, is attending a convention with her husband.

12. The swimmer Mark Spitz won seven gold medals in one Olympics.

13. Fort Worth, a city in Texas, is almost midway between the Atlantic and the Pacific.

14. Aunt Lee, my father's sister, is coming to visit.

15. Mr. Diddon, coach of the hockey team, has never had a losing season.

16. Monticello, Jefferson's home, is an example of colonial architecture.

17. The inventor Thomas Edison is responsible for many electrical breakthroughs.

18. Athens, the leading city of ancient Greece, was a center of culture.

19. The Aztec king Moctezuma II was captured by Cortés.

20. The boll weevil, a small beetle, causes great damage to cotton.

21. Hoover Dam, a dam in the Colorado River, took five years to build.

22. Antares, a star many times larger than the sun, is the red star in Scorpio.

23. The composer Mozart lived a short but productive life.

24. That is a copperhead, one of the four poisonous snakes found in the United States.

25. Mt. McKinley, a rugged mountain, is the tallest mountain in North America.

44

Name _____ Date _____

Verbs

> - A **verb** is a word that expresses action, being, or state of being.
>   EXAMPLES:
>   Alex **traveled** to Europe.
>   Maura **is** an accountant.
> - A verb has four principal parts: **present, present participle, past,** and **past participle.**
> - For regular verbs, form the present participle by adding <u>ing</u> to the present. Use a form of the helping verb <u>be</u> with the present participle.
> - Form the past and past participle by adding <u>ed</u> to the present. Use a form of the helping verb <u>have</u> with the past participle.
>   EXAMPLES:
>
> | Present | Present Participle | Past | Past Participle |
> |---------|--------------------|------|-----------------|
> | listen | (is) listening | listened | (have, has, had) listened |
> | help | (is) helping | helped | (have, has, had) helped |
> | change | (is) changing | changed | (have, has, had) changed |
>
> - Irregular verbs form their past and past participle in other ways. A dictionary shows the principal parts of these verbs.

 Write the present participle, past, and past participle for each verb.

PRESENT	PRESENT PARTICIPLE	PAST	PAST PARTICIPLE
1. scatter	(is) scattering	scattered	(have, had, has) scattered
2. express			
3. paint			
4. call			
5. cook			
6. observe			
7. look			
8. walk			
9. ramble			
10. shout			
11. notice			
12. order			
13. gaze			
14. borrow			
15. start			
16. work			

Language: Usage and Practice 8, SV 1419027859

Verb Phrases

> - A **verb phrase** consists of a main verb and one or more **helping verbs.**
> - A helping verb is also called an **auxiliary verb.**
> - In a verb phrase, the helping verb or verbs precede the main verb.
>   EXAMPLE: Liz **has been** reading a mystery.
> - The helping verbs are:
>   am, are, is, was, were, be, being, been
>   has, have, had
>   do, does, did
>   can, could, must, may, might
>   shall, should, will, would

 Underline each verb or verb phrase and circle each helping verb in the sentences below.

1. Most people have heard the story of Jonathan Chapman.

2. He was born in 1775 and has become an American legend.

3. You may have heard of him as the barefooted, lovable Johnny Appleseed.

4. As Jonathan Chapman, he had grown up in the woods near Boston, Massachusetts.

5. He had learned about fruit trees in the orchards near his family's farm.

6. He was always interested in the stories he had heard about the Great West.

7. As a young man, he had declared, "I will go west to Pennsylvania and plant my own orchard."

8. Jonathan had done just that, but in a few years, the wilderness had moved farther west.

9. "What should I do now?" Jonathan asked himself.

10. "I will plant other apple orchards!" was his answer.

11. Jonathan could not remain content.

12. Soon he was traveling with the other settlers as the frontier pushed farther and farther west.

13. People called him Johnny Appleseed, that odd man who did not have a home.

14. He would sleep out in the open with his beloved trees.

 Use each verb phrase in a sentence.

15. should learn _____

16. will occur _____

17. may find _____

18. have tried _____

19. can make _____

20. will go _____

Language: Usage and Practice 8, SV 1419027859

Verb Tenses

- The **tense** of a verb tells the time of the action or being.
- There are six main tenses: present, past, future, present perfect, past perfect, and future prefect.
- **Present tense** tells about what is happening now.
  - EXAMPLES: Emily **sings.** The kittens **are playing.**
- **Past tense** tells about something that happened in the past.
  - EXAMPLES: Emily **sang** in the play. The kittens **were playing** on the porch.
- **Future tense** tells about something that will happen in the future.
  - EXAMPLES: Emily **will sing** in the play. The kittens **will play** on the porch.
- **Present perfect tense** tells about something that occurred at an indefinite time in the past.
  - EXAMPLE: Emily **has sung** the song.
- **Present perfect tense** is also used to tell about something that began in the past and continues in the present.
  - EXAMPLE: The kittens **have been playing** on the porch.
- **Past perfect tense** tells about something completed at some past time before something else.
  - EXAMPLES: Emily **had sung** before you arrived. The kittens **had been playing** on the porch until Thomas came home.
- **Future perfect tense** tells about something that will be completed before some definite future time.
  - EXAMPLES: Emily **will have finished** singing by eight o'clock.

 Underline each verb or verb phrase. Write <u>present</u>, <u>past</u>, <u>future</u>, <u>present perfect</u>, <u>past perfect</u>, or <u>future perfect</u> to describe the tense.

1. I <u>brought</u> these vegetables. _____ past _____

2. Yes, I know her. _____

3. They will close the office tomorrow. _____

4. The work will continue for several days. _____

5. His friend has donated the painting to the museum. _____

6. Alex had told us many stories about his travels. _____

7. Jesse Owens was a famous track star. _____

8. She sings well. _____

9. Mark will have paid for the meal. _____

10. I will have been in St. Louis for a week. _____

11. The neighborhood children had been playing baseball. _____

12. I have anchored the boat. _____

Language: Usage and Practice 8, SV 1419027859

Using Irregular Verbs

✳ **Write the principal parts of each verb. You may use a dictionary.**

PRESENT	PRESENT PARTICIPLE	PAST	PAST PARTICIPLE
1. do	is doing	did	has done
2. come	_____	_____	_____
3. eat	_____	_____	_____
4. go	_____	_____	_____
5. see	_____	_____	_____
6. take	_____	_____	_____

✳ **Write the correct form of the verb in parentheses to complete each sentence.**

7. (see)   I had never _____ the waterfall before.

8. (see)   Have you ever _____ a helicopter?

9. (take)   Lorie is _____ the hammer with her.

10. (see)   We have just _____ a passenger train going over the bridge.

11. (eat)   Haven't you _____ your lunch?

12. (go)   You should have _____ with us, Neil.

13. (go)   Jaime is _____ to a committee meeting.

14. (eat)   Have you ever _____ a spiced olive?

15. (go)   Julian has _____ to play a video game.

16. (take)   Carey is _____ the photograph now.

17. (do)   Who _____ the landscaping around this building?

18. (do)   We have _____ a great deal of outside reading on the topic for discussion.

19. (take)   Aren't we _____ the wrong road?

20. (come)   People have _____ from every state to see Carlsbad Caverns.

21. (eat)   We had _____ different foods in different areas of the country.

22. (see)   Terrell, you should have _____ the last game.

23. (come)   Most of our people _____ this way on the way to the park.

24. (do)   Matthew _____ his best to beat his own record in the broad jump.

Language: Usage and Practice 8, SV 1419027859

Using Irregular Verbs, p. 2

 Write the principal parts of each verb. You may use a dictionary.

PRESENT	PRESENT PARTICIPLE	PAST	PAST PARTICIPLE
25. begin	_____	_____	_____
26. drink	_____	_____	_____
27. drive	_____	_____	_____
28. give	_____	_____	_____
29. run	_____	_____	_____

Write the correct form of the verb in parentheses to complete each sentence.

30. (give) My friend _____ this poem to me.

31. (run) The excited children _____ down the street.

32. (begin) Work on the new building had _____ this week.

33. (begin) I _____ this project yesterday.

34. (drink) Haven't you _____ some of this delicious fruit juice?

35. (drive) Steven, have you ever _____ a car?

36. (give) Gwendolyn Brooks has _____ us many interesting poems.

37. (begin) The supervisor of the crew is _____ to explain the work orders.

38. (run) Rachel, have you _____ into Aunt Sarah?

39. (run) The girl _____ to meet her parents.

40. (begin) That problem _____ last year.

41. (give) Leonard has _____ me a painting for my living room.

42. (begin) Look, it is _____ to rain.

43. (run) They _____ hard to get out of the rain.

44. (give) Mrs. Williams has _____ me a job in her store.

45. (give) Donna, who _____ you this watch?

46. (begin) We haven't _____ eating all the bananas.

47. (drink) Have you _____ from this cup?

48. (begin) We _____ raking the leaves this morning.

49. (run) Michelle is _____ in the 2-mile race.

Language: Usage and Practice 8, SV 1419027859

More Irregular Verbs

✳ **Write the principal parts of each verb. You may use a dictionary.**

PRESENT	PRESENT PARTICIPLE	PAST	PAST PARTICIPLE
1. grow	_____	_____	_____
2. know	_____	_____	_____
3. ring	_____	_____	_____
4. sing	_____	_____	_____
5. speak	_____	_____	_____

✳ **Write the correct form of the verb in parentheses to complete each sentence.**

6. (sing)   Have you ever _____ a solo?

7. (grow)   In several minutes, my eyes _____ accustomed to the dark.

8. (know)   Bob _____ the answer.

9. (grow)   It has _____ very cold during the last hour.

10. (sing)   Ricardo is _____ although his throat is sore.

11. (ring)   Why hasn't the bell _____?

12. (grow)   Lettuce had first _____ in China.

13. (speak)   Sheryl _____ to Jonathan yesterday.

14. (ring)   The carrier _____ the doorbell.

15. (speak)   Has Rafael _____ to you about his promotion?

16. (speak)   A police officer is _____ to a group of concerned citizens.

17. (sing)   Natalie and her sister _____ on a local TV program last week.

18. (know)   We have _____ the members of that family a long time.

19. (ring)   The mission bells _____ each morning last week.

20. (throw)   Have you _____ away this morning's paper?

21. (grow)   Charles, I believe you have _____ a prize-winning rose.

22. (know)   We have _____ Roberto's brother for three years.

23. (grow)   Because of the rains, the grass is _____ rapidly.

24. (ring)   We _____ the doorbell, but no one answered it.

25. (speak)   Kayla has _____ of you quite often, Jeffrey.

Unit 3: Grammar and Usage
Language: Usage and Practice 8, SV 1419027859

More Irregular Verbs, p. 2

 Write the principal parts of each verb. You may use a dictionary.

PRESENT	PRESENT PARTICIPLE	PAST	PAST PARTICIPLE
26. blow	_____	_____	_____
27. break	_____	_____	_____
28. choose	_____	_____	_____
29. draw	_____	_____	_____
30. fly	_____	_____	_____

Write the correct form of the verb in parentheses to complete each sentence.

31. (draw)   Kim has _____ many cartoons for the daily paper.

32. (blow)   The storm _____ tumbleweeds across the prairie.

33. (fly)   The tiny mockingbird is _____ from its nest.

34. (choose)   We _____ only willing persons for the committee.

35. (choose)   Our club has _____ a motto.

36. (blow)   Has the five o'clock whistle _____?

37. (break)   I accidentally _____ my sister's antique vase.

38. (break)   Her promise had not been _____.

39. (choose)   The coach is _____ the line-up for today's game.

40. (draw)   A famous artist _____ these sketches.

41. (break)   One of the windows in the house had _____ during the storm.

42. (break)   The handle of my hammer _____ while I was using it.

43. (choose)   Has anyone _____ the salad for lunch?

44. (break)   Suzanne _____ this chair yesterday.

45. (freeze)   Those pipes _____ last February.

46. (choose)   Do you think I have _____ wisely?

47. (break)   They _____ our winning streak last week.

48. (draw)   Have you _____ your map, Lew?

49. (break)   Who is _____ these windows?

50. (draw)   Their plans for the new house have been _____.

Language: Usage and Practice 8, SV 1419027859

Even More Irregular Verbs

 Write the principal parts of each verb. You may use a dictionary.

PRESENT	PRESENT PARTICIPLE	PAST	PAST PARTICIPLE
1. become	_____	_____	_____
2. fall	_____	_____	_____
3. ride	_____	_____	_____
4. rise	_____	_____	_____
5. steal	_____	_____	_____
6. show	_____	_____	_____
7. sink	_____	_____	_____
8. swim	_____	_____	_____
9. tear	_____	_____	_____
10. wear	_____	_____	_____

 Write the correct form of the verb in parentheses to complete each sentence.

11. (ride)   Have you ever _____ on a tractor?

12. (rise)   The temperature has _____ ten degrees this afternoon.

13. (wear)   We _____ our sweaters because the night air was very cool.

14. (steal)   Look! Carolyn has _____ third base!

15. (ride)   How far are we _____ today?

16. (swim)   Shonna is _____ around the pool.

17. (tear)   The child _____ his jeans when he fell down.

18. (sink)   When his boat _____, Crusoe was tossed about in the sea.

19. (steal)   Our new car has been _____ this chair yesterday.

20. (ride)   Have you ever _____ in an airplane?

21. (wear)   This wire has almost been _____ in two.

22. (wear)   I have _____ this coat for several winters.

23. (rise)   The river recently _____ beyond the flood stage.

24. (rise)   Diane has _____ from editor to president of the company.

25. (fall)   All the pears have _____ from the tree.

Mood

> - **Mood** is a form of the verb that shows the manner of doing or being.
> - There are three types of moods: indicative, subjunctive, and imperative.
> - **Indicative mood** states a fact or asks a question.
>   - EXAMPLES:
>   - Ben **came** Friday.
>   - How many **went** to the meeting?
> - **Subjunctive mood** can indicate a wish or a contrary-to-fact condition.
> - Use <u>were</u> to express the subjunctive.
>   - EXAMPLE: I would help you, if I **were** able. (I am not able.)
> - **Imperative mood** expresses a command or a request.
>   - EXAMPLES:
>   - **Ask** no more questions.
>   - Let's **start** immediately.

 Write the mood of each underlined word.

1. <u>Come</u> here at once. _____

2. I <u>did</u> not <u>see</u> Carla. _____

3. If I <u>were</u> not so tired, I would go to a movie. _____

4. <u>Call</u> for him at once. _____

5. Where <u>has</u> Brittany <u>moved</u>? _____

6. Who <u>invented</u> the sewing machine? _____

7. Juanita <u>came</u> Saturday. _____

8. Patrick wishes it <u>were</u> true. _____

9. <u>Come</u> here, Jennifer. _____

10. I wish it <u>were</u> summer. _____

11. <u>Be</u> home early. _____

12. <u>Ring</u> the bell immediately. _____

13. The members of the band <u>sold</u> birthday calendars. _____

14. If I <u>were</u> you, I'd stop that. _____

15. Zack <u>likes</u> my new sweater. _____

16. My friends <u>painted</u> the entire house. _____

17. If this <u>were</u> a sunny day, I would go with you. _____

18. <u>Tell</u> us where you went. _____

19. He greeted me as though I <u>were</u> a stranger. _____

Transitive and Intransitive Verbs

> - There are two kinds of action verbs: transitive and intransitive.
> - A **transitive verb** has a direct object.
>   EXAMPLE: Columbus **discovered** America.
> - An **intransitive verb** does not need an object to complete its meaning.
> - Linking verbs are always intransitive.
>   EXAMPLES:
>   The wind **howled.**
>   He **is** afraid.

 Underline each verb and classify it as transitive or intransitive.

1. We walked into the new school. _____ intransitive _____

2. Ornithology is the study of birds. _____

3. Move those blocks now! _____

4. Everyone listened carefully. _____

5. The workers wore special uniforms. _____

6. We built a barbecue pit in our backyard. _____

7. What is the name of this picture? _____

8. He lives in Germany. _____

9. Who appointed the principal of Stuart High? _____

10. Leroy paid the bill. _____

11. We send many good customers to them. _____

12. London is the capital city of Great Britain. _____

13. Frank drew many excellent cartoons. _____

14. We study hard for tests. _____

15. The frightened children cried loudly. _____

16. Lora made this poster. _____

17. Thousands of people ran in the race. _____

18. We learned three new songs. _____

19. The stray dogs barked. _____

20. Please bring me a book about famous Canadian scientists. _____

21. Evelyn baked a lemon meringue pie. _____

Language: Usage and Practice 8, SV 1419027859

Transitive and Intransitive Verbs, p. 2

✳ **Underline each verb or verb phrase and classify it as transitive or intransitive.**

22. The President of the United States signed the new law. _____

23. The workers repaired the telephone lines. _____

24. The factory shipped the shoes. _____

25. Wasteful cutting of timber may cause a shortage of lumber. _____

26. Wolf was Rip Van Winkle's sole friend. _____

27. The city of Mobile, Alabama, has a wonderful harbor. _____

28. Explain your meaning, please. _____

29. The wind whistled down the chimney. _____

30. The heavy floods blocked traffic for miles. _____

31. Many leaves have dropped in our yard. _____

32. Inventions change our way of living. _____

33. Birmingham, England, attracts many tourists. _____

34. Dorothea Lange was a famous photographer. _____

35. Julio has a fine collection of coins. _____

36. Who invented the lightning rod? _____

37. We cooked our steaks over an open fire. _____

38. Madame Curie discovered radium. _____

39. Gene traveled through North America and South America. _____

40. Cole Porter composed "Night and Day." _____

41. Amelia Earhart was a famous pilot. _____

42. The tornado destroyed several stores. _____

43. Derrek exercises every day. _____

44. We talked for hours. _____

45. Have you ever seen Plymouth Rock? _____

46. Abandoned campfires often cause great forest fires. _____

47. He is studying hard for the exam. _____

48. The United States bought Alaska in 1867. _____

Language: Usage and Practice 8, SV 1419027859

Active and Passive Voice

> * **Voice** refers to the relation of a subject to the action expressed by the verb.
> * In the **active voice,** the subject does the action.
>   EXAMPLE: The club members **made** these decorations.
> * In the **passive voice,** the subject is acted upon.
>   EXAMPLE: These decorations **were made** by the club members.
> * Only transitive verbs can be used in the passive voice.

✿ **Underline each verb. Then write active or passive to identify its voice.**

__passive__ 1. The phonograph was invented by Edison.

_____ 2. Tara hit a home run.

_____ 3. The bell was rung by the caretaker.

_____ 4. The football was thrown out of bounds.

_____ 5. Ricardo has bought some new fishing tackle.

_____ 6. The decision of the committee was announced yesterday.

_____ 7. Doug blamed Pamela for making him late.

_____ 8. The first three people were selected for the job openings.

_____ 9. Carlo typed the letter.

_____ 10. Angela quickly stated the reason for not attending.

_____ 11. Andrew flopped into the chair.

_____ 12. Many songs were written by Stephen Foster.

_____ 13. The police officer gave me a ticket.

_____ 14. Dr. Koneru held a press conference.

_____ 15. Rosa has bought a new car.

_____ 16. His heart was broken by the cruelty of his friends.

_____ 17. Senator Dale shook their hands.

_____ 18. The boat was carried to the landing.

_____ 19. The party was given for her birthday.

_____ 20. Eva wrote the winning essay.

Gerunds

> • A **gerund** is the present participle of a verb form ending in <u>ing</u> that is used as a noun.
> • A gerund may be the subject, direct object, or object of a preposition.
>   EXAMPLES:
>   **Exercising** is vital to good health. (subject)
>   Tanya enjoys **exercising**. (direct object)
>   I have thought of **exercising**. (object of preposition)

 Underline each gerund.

1. We enjoy <u>living</u> on the farm.

2. Airplanes are used in fighting forest fires.

3. Landing an airplane requires skill.

4. Climbing Pikes Peak is quite an experience.

5. The moaning of the wind through the pines lulled me to sleep.

6. The dog's barking awakened everyone in the house.

7. Keeping his temper is difficult for John.

8. Sue Li objected to our hanging the picture in this room.

9. Laughing aloud is encouraged by the comedian.

10. Being treasurer of this club is a responsibility.

11. Making a speech makes me nervous.

12. Winning this game will place our soccer team first in the league.

13. It was my first attempt at pitching horseshoes.

14. Rapid eating will make digestion difficult.

15. Playing golf is a favorite pastime in many countries.

16. Planning a party requires much thought.

17. We have completed our packing for the trip to the mountains.

18. The howling of the dogs disturbed our sleep.

19. I am tired of doing this work.

20. We are fond of living here.

21. Native Americans once spent much time planting, hunting, and fishing.

22. Neat writing is important in school.

23. I enjoy skating on this pond.

24. Jason taught us the rules of boating.

25. Pressing the wrong button can be very dangerous.

26. Airplanes are used in the mapping of large areas.

27. Swimming in this lake is my favorite sport.

28. I enjoy driving a car.

Infinitives

> • An **infinitive** is the base form of the verb, commonly preceded by to.
> • An infinitive may be used as a noun, adverb, or adjective.
>   EXAMPLES:
>   **To know** him is **to like** him. (noun)
>   She came here **to study**. (adverb)
>   That is the movie **to see**. (adjective)

 Underline each infinitive.

1. I want to go home before it gets any colder.

2. We went to see the play while Emilio was here.

3. I prepared the salad to serve for lunch.

4. To shoot firecrackers in the city limits is against the law in some places.

5. I like to walk in the country.

6. They were taught to stand, to sit, to walk, and to dance gracefully.

7. Gradually people learned to use fire and to make tools.

8. I need to get a new coat.

9. We plan to make the trip in four hours.

10. Karol, are you too tired to clean the kitchen?

11. Adam, try to be on time in the morning.

12. Ron plans to travel in Canada during August.

13. Who taught you to play golf?

14. We were taught to rise early.

15. We were hoping to see you at the reunion.

16. Pay one fee to enter the amusement park.

17. Britney, I forgot to mail your package.

18. To cook this turkey will require several hours.

19. The children ran to meet their friend.

20. We are learning to speak Spanish.

21. We are planning to exhibit our artwork next week.

22. To succeed as an artist was Rick's dream.

23. We went to see the parade.

24. We are ready to eat.

25. It was easy to see the reason for that actor's popularity.

26. The only way to have a friend is to be one.

27. Madame Curie was the only woman to receive the Nobel Prize a second time.

28. To score the most points is the object of the game.

29. We need to go grocery shopping.

30. Do you want to paint the fence on Saturday?

Participles

> • A **present participle** or a **past participle** is a verb form that may be used as an adjective.
>   EXAMPLES:
>   A **dripping** faucet can be a nuisance.
>   **Wilted** flowers were removed from the vase.

 Underline each participle.

1. We saw a running deer in the forest.
2. The chart showing sales figures is very helpful.
3. The scampering cat ran to the nearest tree.
4. A team of deep-sea divers discovered the hidden treasure.
5. We saw the thunderstorm advancing across the plains.
6. Biting insects hovered over our campsite at night.
7. His foot, struck by the falling timbers, was injured.
8. The whispering pines filled the air with their fresh scent.
9. People preparing for a career in aviation should master mathematics.
10. We drove slowly, enjoying every minute of the drive.
11. Onions are among the largest vegetable crops produced in the United States.
12. The truck, burdened with its load, traveled slowly over the rough road.
13. Janna, thinking about her new job, was very happy.
14. Several passengers injured in the wreck were brought to the local hospital.
15. That expanding city will soon be the largest one in the state.
16. The fire, fanned by the high winds, threatened the entire area.
17. The rude person, shoving others aside, went to see the manager.
18. The lake, frozen solidly, looked like a huge mirror.
19. The man playing the trombone is my brother.
20. The cleaned apartment was ready for new tenants.
21. Teasing children ran at Rip Van Winkle's heels.
22. Balloons lifting weather instruments are released daily by many weather stations.
23. The chirping bird flew from tree to tree.
24. The surviving pilot described the accident.
25. The dedicated artist worked patiently.
26. Homing pigeons were used in the experiment.
27. The whistling youngster skipped happily down the road.
28. Ironed shirts were stacked neatly at the cleaners.
29. Those standing near the fence should form a second line.
30. The child ran to his loving father, who comforted him.

Language: Usage and Practice 8, SV 1419027859

Name _____ Date _____

Using *Lie/Lay*

> - The verb <u>lie</u> means "to recline" or "to occupy a certain place." It does not take an object.
>   EXAMPLE: The baby is **lying** in her crib.
> - The verb <u>lay</u> means "to place." It takes an object.
>   EXAMPLE: **Lay** the plates on the shelf.
> - The following are forms of <u>lie</u> and <u>lay</u>:
>
> | Present | Present Participle | Past | Past Participle |
> |---------|--------------------|------|-----------------|
> | lie | lying | lay | (have) lain |
> | lay | laying | laid | (have) laid |

 Circle the correct word in parentheses to complete each sentence.

1. Canada (lays, lies) to the north of the United States.

2. (Lay, Lie) these books on the table.

3. My cat was (laying, lying) on the floor.

4. Stuart likes to (lay, lie) in the shade.

5. Jarred (lay, laid) the morning paper by his plate.

6. She (lay, laid) the letter on the table.

7. I have (lain, laid) awake for hours the last two nights.

8. He is not able to (lay, lie) on his left side.

9. Teri (lay, laid) her book aside and went to the door.

10. Where (lies, lays) the land to which these ships are going?

11. The dogs had (laid, lain) under the porch all night.

12. I (lay, laid) a long time beside the swimming pool.

13. California (lays, lies) to the east of the Pacific Ocean.

 Write four sentences, each with a different form of <u>lie</u>. Write four sentences, each with a different form of <u>lay</u>.

14. _____

15. _____

16. _____

17. _____

18. _____

19. _____

20. _____

21. _____

Language: Usage and Practice 8, SV 1419027859

Name _____ Date _____

Using *Sit/Set* and *Learn/Teach*

> - The verb <u>sit</u> means "to take a resting position."
>   - EXAMPLE: Please **sit** in that chair.
> - The verb <u>set</u> means "to place."
>   - EXAMPLE: **Set** the cups on the saucers.
> - The verb <u>learn</u> means "to acquire knowledge."
>   - EXAMPLE: I want to **learn** how to tap-dance.
> - The verb <u>teach</u> means "to give knowledge to" or "to instruct."
>   - EXAMPLE: Please **teach** me to tap-dance.
>
> | Present | Present Participle | Past | Past Participle |
> |---------|--------------------|------|-----------------|
> | sit | sitting | sat | (have) sat |
> | set | setting | set | (have) set |
> | learn | learning | learned | (have) learned |
> | teach | teaching | taught | (have) taught |

 Circle the correct word in parentheses to complete each sentence.

1. Please (sit, set) this table on the patio.

2. My friend is (learning, teaching) us to swim this summer.

3. You should (learn, teach) to eat more slowly.

4. Where do you prefer to (sit, set)?

5. The little dog is always found (sitting, setting) by its owner.

6. Such an experience should (learn, teach) you a lesson.

7. In a theater I always like to (sit, set) near the aisle.

8. I (sat, set) in a reserved seat at the last game.

9. Let me (learn, teach) you a shorter way to do this.

10. Alberto, please (sit, set) down on the step.

11. If you (learn, teach) me how to play tennis, I'll try to (learn, teach) well.

12. With tired sighs, we (sat, set) down on the couch.

13. Andy, have you (sit, set) out the plants?

14. Michael, did you (learn, teach) your dog all these tricks?

15. We watched the workers as they (sat, set) stone upon stone.

16. Marcy has (learned, taught) me to water-ski.

17. You can (learn, teach) some animals more easily than others.

18. Mona, do you like to (sit, set) by the window?

19. The first-aid course has (learned, taught) me important procedures.

20. Who (learned, taught) you how to ride a bike?

21. Please (sit, set) these chairs on the rug.

22. Manuel has (sat, set) his work aside.

23. Claire is (learning, teaching) children how to sail in August.

24. All the students are (sitting, setting) quietly.

Language: Usage and Practice 8, SV 1419027859

Pronouns

- A **pronoun** is a word used in place of a noun.
- A **personal pronoun** is chosen based on the way it is used in the sentence.
- A **subject pronoun** is used in the subject of a sentence and after a linking verb.
    EXAMPLES:
        He is a chemist.
        The chemist is **he**.
- An **object pronoun** is used after an action verb or a preposition.
    EXAMPLES:
        Jan gave **me** the gift.
        Jan gave the gift to **me**.
- A **possessive pronoun** is used to show ownership of something.
    EXAMPLES:
        The new car is **ours**.
        That is **our** car.

 Underline each pronoun.

1. Brian, do you have my ticket to the play?
2. Just between you and me, I want to go with them.
3. Ed, will you help me carry our trunk?
4. May I go with you?
5. We saw him standing in line to go to a movie.
6. Just be sure to find Candace and me.
7. We will be ready when they come for us.
8. She sent this box of frozen steaks to Andrea and me.
9. She asked you and me to be on her bowling team.
10. We saw them go into the building on the corner.
11. Last week we sent flowers to our sick friend.
12. He must choose their dinner.
13. She is my English instructor.
14. They have never invited us to go with them.
15. The first-place winner is she.
16. Can he compete against you?
17. She made the dinner for us.
18. Liza and I are going on vacation in June.
19. Where is your umbrella?
20. Sharon gave me a book to read.
21. Do you know where our cottage is?
22. If I lend you my car, will you take care of it?
23. I gave him my word that we would visit her.
24. When they saw us fishing, Rob and Diane changed their clothes.
25. Your toes are peeking through your socks.
26. Marie showed us how to fasten her bike to our car.

Name _____ Date _____

Using *Its* and *It's*

> • It's is a contraction for "it is."
>   EXAMPLE: **It's** a beautiful day.
> • Its is a personal pronoun.
>   EXAMPLE: The dog hurt **its** leg.

 Underline the correct word in parentheses to complete each sentence.

1. Our town is proud of (its, it's) elected officials.
2. (Its, It's) time for the curtain to rise.
3. Tell me when (its, it's) time for that television program.
4. (Its, It's) a mile from our house to the grocery store.
5. I think (its, it's) too cold to walk.
6. (Its, It's) almost time for the show to start.
7. (Its, It's) noon already.
8. (Its, It's) time to give the puppy (its, it's) bath.
9. The cat is playing with (its, it's) toy.
10. (Its, It's) time for us to start home.
11. It looks like (its, it's) going to rain.
12. This dog has lost (its, it's) collar.
13. I think that bird has hurt (its, it's) wing.
14. I do believe (its, it's) getting colder.
15. The dog is looking for (its, it's) owner.
16. (Its, It's) a long and very interesting story.
17. Did you know (its, it's) color was green?
18. The pony shook (its, it's) head and ran to the stable.
19. Do you think (its, it's) too late to call?
20. The bear cub imitated (its, it's) mother.

 Write three sentences of your own in which you use _its_.

21. _____
22. _____
23. _____

 Write three sentences of your own in which you use _it's_.

24. _____
25. _____
26. _____

Language: Usage and Practice 8, SV 1419027859

Name _____ Date _____

Demonstrative and Indefinite Pronouns

- A **demonstrative pronoun** is used to point out a specific person or thing.
- This and that are used in place of singular nouns. <u>This</u> refers to a person or thing nearby, and <u>that</u> refers to a person or thing farther away.
  - EXAMPLES:
    - **This** is mine.
    - **That** is the right one.
- These and those are used in place of plural nouns. <u>These</u> points to persons or things nearby, and <u>those</u> points to persons or things farther away.
  - EXAMPLES:
    - **These** are the best ones.
    - **Those** don't look ripe.

 Underline each demonstrative pronoun.

1. Those are the books I lost.
2. That is where Angelina lives.
3. I'm not sure these are my scissors.
4. This is my pen; that is Pat's book.
5. I think those are interesting books.
6. Is that your first mistake?
7. This is Gretchen's time card.
8. Give these to your friend.

9. These are Lily's shoes.
10. Please don't mention this.
11. I think those are just rumors.
12. Will this be our last chance?
13. Dave, those are your messages.
14. These are large peaches.
15. Sorry, that was my last piece.
16. Who told you that?

- An **indefinite pronoun** does not refer to a specific person or thing.
  - EXAMPLE: **Many** are called, but **few** are chosen.
- The indefinite pronouns <u>anybody</u>, <u>anyone</u>, <u>anything</u>, <u>each</u>, <u>everyone</u>, <u>everybody</u>, <u>everything</u>, <u>nobody</u>, <u>no one</u>, <u>nothing</u>, <u>one</u>, <u>somebody</u>, <u>someone</u>, and <u>something</u> are singular. They take singular verbs.
  - EXAMPLE: **Everyone is** ready.
- The indefinite pronouns <u>both</u>, <u>few</u>, <u>many</u>, <u>several</u>, and <u>some</u> are plural. They take plural verbs.
  - EXAMPLE: **Several are** ready.

 Underline each indefinite pronoun.

17. Both worked hard.
18. Let each help decorate.
19. Several have called about the job.
20. Unfortunately, some never learn.
21. Everyone was delighted at our party.
22. I think someone forgot this sweater.
23. Some asked for pens.
24. He thinks that each is right.

25. Has anyone seen my wallet?
26. Will someone wash the dishes?
27. Both of the singers are here.
28. One is absent.
29. Each must carry a bag.
30. Some always succeed.
31. Did someone leave this lunch?
32. Everybody is to be here early.

     Unit 3: Grammar and Usage
Language: Usage and Practice 8, SV 1419027859

Name _____   Date _____

Antecedents

> • An **antecedent** is the word to which a pronoun refers.
>   EXAMPLE: **Stars** are lovely when **they** shine.
> • A pronoun must agree with its antecedent in **gender** (masculine, feminine, or neuter) and **number** (singular or plural).
>   EXAMPLES:
>   **Susan** helped **her** friend.
>   The **people** went in **their** cars.
> • If the antecedent is an indefinite pronoun, it is correct to use a masculine pronoun. However, it is now common to use both a masculine and feminine pronoun.
>   EXAMPLES:
>   Someone lost **his** dog.
>   Someone lost **his or her** dog.

 Underline the correct pronoun in parentheses and circle its antecedent.

1. Everyone should work hard at (their, his or her) job.
2. Each of the children willingly did (his or her, their) share of the camp duties.
3. Sophia gave me (her, their) coat to wear.
4. I took (my, our) friend to the ceremony.
5. All members were asked to bring (his or her, their) contributions today.
6. The women have had (her, their) vacation.
7. Someone has left (her or his, their) automobile across the driveway.
8. If each does (his or her, their) best, our chorus will win.
9. Would you tell Joanne that (her, his) soup is ready?
10. Every woman did (her, their) best to make the program a success.
11. Never judge anyone entirely by (his or her, their) looks.
12. Each student should do (his or her, their) own work.
13. I lost one of (my, our) favorite earrings at the dance.
14. Each woman takes (her, their) own equipment on the camping trip.
15. Each one has a right to (his or her, their) own opinion in this matter.
16. (His, Her) sense of humor is what I like best about Joseph.
17. Some man has left (his, their) raincoat.
18. The two waiters dropped (his, their) trays when they bumped into each other.
19. Has each student received (his or her, their) report card?
20. Every person is expected to do (her or his, their) best.
21. We knew that every man at the meeting expressed (his, their) opinion.
22. Every woman furnishes (her, their) own transportation.
23. Jeff and Tom found (his, their) cabin in the dark.
24. Cliff brings his dog every time (he, she) visits.
25. The bird was in (their, its) nest.
26. Mark read (his, her) final essay for me.

Language: Usage and Practice 8, SV 1419027859

Relative Pronouns

> - A **relative pronoun** is a pronoun that can introduce a subordinate clause.
> - The relative pronouns are <u>who</u>, <u>whom</u>, <u>whose</u> (referring to persons), <u>which</u> (referring to things), and <u>that</u> (referring to persons or things).
> - A subordinate clause, when introduced by a relative pronoun, serves as an adjective. It modifies a word, or antecedent, in the main clause.
>   EXAMPLES:
>   Kimberly knows the author **whose** articles we read in class.
>   The family for **whom** I work is from Canada.
>   The movie **that** won the prize is playing.

 Underline each relative pronoun and circle its antecedent.

1. The letter that was published in our daily paper was very long.

2. It was Kara who sang the most difficult song.

3. Robert Burns, who wrote "My Heart's in the Highlands," was Scottish.

4. It was Sylvia who wanted Zach's address.

5. The shop that was filled with video games is going out of business.

6. My parents live in a New England farmhouse that was built many years ago.

7. This is the pearl that is so valuable.

8. The bridge, which is made of wood, was built two hundred years ago.

9. Did you see the animal that ran across the road?

10. Good roads have opened up many regions that were formerly impassable.

11. For our Thanksgiving dinner, we had a turkey that weighed twenty pounds.

12. This story, which was written by Eudora Welty, is most interesting.

13. Anna is a person whom you can trust.

14. We ate the delicious hamburgers that Harrison had prepared.

15. Food that is eaten in pleasant surroundings is usually digested easily.

16. This is the first painting that I did.

17. The sweater that you want is too expensive.

18. She is the one whom we watched at the track meet.

19. The only money that they spent was for food.

20. Your friend is one person who is inconsiderate.

21. A rare animal that lives in our city zoo was featured on the evening news.

22. Heather is one of the guests whom I invited.

23. Is this the file for which you've been searching?

24. Leonardo da Vinci is the artist whose work they most admire.

25. The science museum is an attraction that is visited by many tourists.

26. Charles Dickens is a writer whose works I've read extensively.

Name _____ Date _____

Using *Who/Whom*

```
• Use who as a subject pronoun.
    EXAMPLE:  Who is your favorite singer?
• Use whom as an object pronoun.
    EXAMPLE:  Whom did Karen call?
    By rearranging the sentence (Karen did call whom?), you can see that
    whom follows the verb and functions as the object.
• Whom can also function as the object of a preposition.
    EXAMPLE:  For whom are you looking?
```

 Complete each sentence with who or whom.

1. _____ told you about our plans?

2. _____ is our greatest living scientist?

3. _____ did Armando send for?

4. _____ are those women?

5. _____ is your instructor?

6. _____ is your friend?

7. To _____ is that package addressed?

8. For _____ shall I ask?

9. _____ do you think can take my place?

10. From _____ did you borrow that costume?

11. _____ have the people elected?

12. _____ does she look like?

13. With _____ do you plan to study?

14. _____ is the new employee?

15. _____ do I resemble, my mother or my father?

16. The person _____ I called is my sister.

17. For _____ is this letter?

18. _____ will we select?

19. _____ told us about Frank?

20. _____ did he call?

21. _____ sat next to me?

Language: Usage and Practice 8, SV 1419027859

Using Pronouns

 Underline the correct pronouns to complete the sentences.

1. It was (I, me) who brought the telegram.

2. (He, Him) and (I, me) are friends.

3. She used a sentence (who, that) contained a clause.

4. Neither (he, him) nor (she, her) was to blame.

5. Megan, will you sit between Dana and (I, me)?

6. The person (who, which) taught us how to swim has moved.

7. (Who, Whom) do you want?

8. Between you and (I, me), I do not believe that rumor.

9. I was not the only person (who, whom) she helped.

10. Lupe, please let Caria and (I, me) go with you.

11. For (who, whom) did Joanne knit this sweater?

12. A misunderstanding arose between (she, her) and (I, me).

13. Did you and (she, her) speak to (he, him) about the meeting?

14. The doctor (who, which) examined the sick child was very gentle.

15. That is a fox, and (them, those) are coyotes.

16. Is that (she, her) in your car?

17. Cal invited Zachary and (I, me) to go swimming.

18. Everyone will write (his or her, their) name.

19. Between you and (I, me), I am disappointed.

20. (Those, That) are my books.

21. Patricia chose you and (I, me).

22. Have you ever played tennis with Brendon and (he, him)?

23. (These, This) are very expensive.

24. It is (he, him) who always plans our refreshments.

25. Were Chip and (he, him) ill yesterday?

26. (Those, That) are the singers we want to hear.

27. Our boss will tell Angelo and (I, me).

28. Was it (he, him) who won the prize?

29. The person (who, whom) we met comes from Brazil.

30. Both want (his or her, their) papers.

31. (Who, Whom) walked three miles this morning?

32. Was it (she, her) who called this morning?

33. No one should comb (his or her, their) hair in public.

34. I thanked the woman (who, whom) helped me.

Adjectives

- An **adjective** is a word that modifies a noun or a pronoun.
  EXAMPLE: He has **red** hair.
- A **descriptive adjective** usually tells what kind, which one, or how many.
  EXAMPLES: **dreary** weather, **this** camera, **two** tickets
- A **proper adjective** is an adjective that is formed from a proper noun. It always begins with a capital letter.
  EXAMPLES: **Canadian** history, **Mexican** food
- The articles <u>a</u>, <u>an</u>, and <u>the</u> are called **limiting adjectives**.

 Underline each adjective.

1. The old delicatessen sells fabulous Greek pastries.

2. The little dog is a very affectionate pet.

3. The weary traveler lay down upon the soft, green turf.

4. The storm was accompanied by a magnificent display of vivid lightning.

5. Every motorist should have good eyes, good ears, and good judgment.

6. Every child in the United States knows about the famous ride of Paul Revere.

7. Fleecy, white clouds were floating overhead.

8. On every side were lofty peaks.

9. We have many clear, bright days in December.

10. Washington was a person of courage and honor.

11. The beautiful memorial fountain was placed near the main entrance of the city park.

12. Cautious movements are required in dangerous areas.

13. Alaska, with its fertile soil, extensive forests, and valuable mines, is a great state.

14. He has a massive head, a broad, deep brow, and large, black eyes.

15. The rain dashed against the windows with a dreary sound.

16. Exercise should be a part of your daily routine.

17. The main street is bordered by stately elms.

18. Show a friendly attitude toward your classmates.

19. The second seat in the fourth row is broken.

20. The bright, colorful leaves of the maple make a wonderful sight in autumn.

21. The old, dusty books were donated to the library.

22. Yellow and green parrots talked to the curious children.

23. The steaming blueberry pie was set on the table.

24. An elegant woman stepped out of the black limousine.

25. Can you hear the chirping baby robins?

26. The salesperson waited on the first customer in line.

Adjectives, p. 2

❋ **Form a proper adjective from each proper noun and use it in a sentence. You may use a dictionary.**

27. Puerto Rico _____

28. Ireland _____

29. South America _____

30. Britain _____

31. France _____

32. Rome _____

33. Canada _____

34. England _____

35. Russia _____

❋ **Write three adjectives to describe each noun.**

36. a friend _____   _____

37. a TV program _____   _____

38. a book _____   _____

39. a sunset _____   _____

40. a conversation _____   _____

41. a soldier _____   _____

42. a party _____   _____

43. a pet _____   _____

44. a child _____   _____

45. a tree _____   _____

❋ **Write two adjectives that could be substituted for the following common adjectives.**

46. pretty _____   _____

47. little _____   _____

48. smart _____   _____

49. big _____   _____

50. nice _____   _____

51. good _____   _____

Language: Usage and Practice 8, SV 1419027859

Demonstrative Adjectives

> - A **demonstrative adjective** is one that points out a specific person or thing.
> - This and that modify singular nouns. This points to a person or thing nearby, and that points to a person or thing farther away.
>   EXAMPLES:
>   **This** pasta is delicious!
>   **That** road will lead us to town.
> - These and those describe plural nouns. These points to people or things nearby, and those points to people or things farther away.
>   EXAMPLES:
>   **These** sunglasses are very stylish.
>   **Those** plants grow well in shady areas.
> - The word them is a pronoun. Never use it to describe a noun.

 Underline the correct word in parentheses to complete each sentence.

1. Please hand me one of (those, them) pencils.

2. Who are (those, them) people?

3. Was your report made from (these, them) articles?

4. Have you heard (those, them) harmonica players?

5. (These, Them) ten problems are very difficult.

6. I do not like (that, those) loud music.

7. I like (this, these) kind of soft lead pencil.

8. (Those, Them) shoes are too small for you.

9. Where did you buy (those, them) cantaloupes?

10. Most people like (that, those) kind of mystery story.

11. Please look carefully for (those, them) receipts.

12. Shannon, please take your brother (these, them) books.

13. (Those, Them) advertisements are very confusing.

14. (Those, Them) buildings are not open to the public.

15. Where did you find (that, those) uniform?

16. Please seat (these, them) guests.

17. Rich lives in (this, these) building.

18. (Those, Them) actors were exceptionally convincing in their roles.

19. Kelly, I sent you (that, these) brochure you requested.

20. Did you see (this, those) new outfits in the store?

21. Mark and Melissa painted (this, these) scenery.

22. (Those, Them) computer programs have been quite helpful.

23. Angie, would you like to read (these, them) memos?

24. (This, These) pair of sandals feels comfortable.

25. Is (that, those) the correct phone number?

Comparing with Adjectives

- An adjective has three degrees of comparison: positive, comparative, and superlative.
- The simple form of an adjective is called the **positive degree.**
  - EXAMPLE: Corey is **happy.**
- When two people or things are being compared, the **comparative degree** is used.
  - EXAMPLE: Corey is **happier** than Katya.
- When three or more people or things are being compared, the **superlative degree** is used.
  - EXAMPLE: Corey is the **happiest** person I know.
- For all adjectives of one syllable and a few adjectives of two syllables, add er to form the comparative degree and est to form the superlative degree.
  - EXAMPLE: tall—taller—tallest
- For some adjectives of two syllables and all adjectives of three or more syllables, use more or less to form the comparative and most or least to form the superlative.
  - EXAMPLES:
    - He is **more educated** than I remember.
    - That is the **most beautiful** horse on the farm.
    - Yoko is **less active** than Mason.
    - Brooke is the **least active** of all.
- Some adjectives have irregular comparisons.
  - EXAMPLES: good, better, best   bad, worse, worst

Write the comparative and superlative forms of each adjective.

POSITIVE	COMPARATIVE	SUPERLATIVE
1. gentle	_____	_____
2. helpful	_____	_____
3. difficult	_____	_____
4. troublesome	_____	_____
5. high	_____	_____
6. delicious	_____	_____
7. intelligent	_____	_____
8. soft	_____	_____

Complete each sentence, using the correct degree of comparison for each adjective in parentheses.

9. (difficult)   This is the _____ problem I have ever faced.

10. (lovely)   A rose is _____ than its thorns.

11. (agreeable)   Ann is _____ in the morning than in the evening.

Language: Usage and Practice 8, SV 1419027859

Adverbs

- An **adverb** is a word that modifies a verb, an adjective, or another adverb.
  EXAMPLES:
  Kellin spoke **casually**.
  Carmen's attitude is **very** positive.
  We did the job **too** carelessly.
- An adverb usually tells how, when, where, to what extent, or how often.
- Many adverbs end in <u>ly</u>.

 Underline each adverb in the sentences below.

1. Preventive medicine has advanced rapidly.

2. The surface of the lake is very quiet.

3. Slowly and surely the tortoise won the race.

4. Afterward the child slept soundly.

5. Tom Sawyer's fence was carefully and thoroughly whitewashed.

6. The horse ran gracefully through the woods.

7. Slowly but steadily the river rose.

8. Jane, you read too rapidly.

9. Leena always dresses stylishly and neatly.

10. The driver turned quickly and abruptly.

11. Was the firefighter seriously injured?

12. Cydney was extremely cautious as she moved slowly away from the danger.

13. Always try to speak correctly and clearly.

14. The assistant typed rapidly.

15. She came in very quietly.

16. Julio worked patiently and carefully.

17. We searched everywhere.

18. Our holidays passed too quickly.

19. The giant airplane landed gently.

20. We looked here, there, and everywhere for Amelia's lost ring.

21. Come here immediately!

22. The flags were waving gaily everywhere.

23. Slowly the long freight train climbed the steep grade.

24. Overhead the stars twinkled brightly.

25. Wash your hands thoroughly before eating.

26. Scott caught the ball and speedily passed it to his teammate.

27. Carefully check every belt and hose in the car.

28. They were quite late.

29. He sees too many movies.

Comparing with Adverbs

> - An adverb has three degrees of comparison: positive, comparative, and superlative.
> - The simple form of the adverb is called the **positive degree.**
>   EXAMPLE: Alex worked **hard** on his project.
> - When two actions are being compared, the **comparative degree** is used.
>   EXAMPLE: Alex worked **harder** than Justin.
> - When three or more actions are being compared, the **superlative degree** is used.
>   EXAMPLE: Alex worked the **hardest** of all.
> - Use er to form the comparative degree and use est to form the superlative degree of one-syllable adverbs.
> - Use more and most with longer adverbs and with adverbs that end in ly.
>   EXAMPLE:
>   Karen finished **more quickly** than Sara.
>   Sara works the **most carefully** of all.
> - Some adverbs have irregular comparative and superlative degrees.
>   EXAMPLES: well, better, best   badly, worse, worst

Write the comparative and superlative form of each adverb.

POSITIVE	COMPARATIVE	SUPERLATIVE
1. fast	_____	_____
2. carefully	_____	_____
3. quietly	_____	_____
4. slow	_____	_____
5. frequently	_____	_____
6. proudly	_____	_____
7. evenly	_____	_____
8. long	_____	_____

 Complete each sentence using the correct degree of comparison for each adverb in parentheses. Some of the forms are irregular.

9. (seriously)   Does Angela take her job _____ than Bette?

10. (high)   Which of the kites flew _____?

11. (thoroughly)   Who cleaned his plate _____, Juan or Bruce?

12. (badly)   This is the _____ I've ever done on a test.

13. (diligently)   Carl works _____ than Mario!

14. (well)   Lisa skis the _____ of everyone in her family.

74

Using Adjectives and Adverbs

 Underline the correct word in parentheses to complete each sentence.

1. Always drive very (careful, carefully).

2. The lake seems (calm, calmly) today.

3. The storm raged (furious, furiously).

4. The dog waited (patient, patiently) for its owner.

5. Nicole's letters are always (cheerful, cheerfully) written.

6. Although our team played (good, well), we lost the game.

7. Always answer your mail (prompt, promptly).

8. Jasper speaks (respectful, respectfully) to everyone.

9. Tara is (happy, happily) with her new work.

10. Write this address (legible, legibly).

11. The time passed (slow, slowly).

12. The robin chirped (happy, happily) from its nest.

13. We were (sure, surely) glad to hear from him.

14. Rebecca tries to do her work (good, well).

15. I think Brandy will (easy, easily) win that contest.

16. We had to talk (loud, loudly) to be heard.

17. Yesterday the sun shone (bright, brightly) all day.

18. He says he sleeps (good, well) every night.

19. The elevator went up (quick, quickly) to the top floor.

20. The storm began very (sudden, suddenly).

21. You did react very (cautious, cautiously).

22. Every student should do this work (accurate, accurately).

23. Eric rode his bike (furious, furiously) to get home on time.

24. The paint on the house is (new, newly).

25. The mist fell (steady, steadily) all evening.

26. The river looked (beautiful, beautifully) in the moonlight.

27. The salesperson always answers questions (courteous, courteously).

28. He always does (good, well) when selling that product.

29. Ryan can swim (good, well).

30. I was (real, really) excited about going to San Francisco.

31. I think he talks (foolish, foolishly).

32. It seems (foolish, foolishly) to me.

33. That bell rang too (loud, loudly) for this small room.

34. Our grass seems to grow very (rapid, rapidly).

Prepositions and Prepositional Phrases

- A **preposition** is a word that shows the relationship of a noun or a pronoun to another word in the sentence.

  EXAMPLES:

  I saw her coming **around** the **corner**.
  She placed the present **on** the **chair**.

- These are some commonly used prepositions:

about	against	at	between	from	of	through	until
above	along	before	by	in	off	to	up
across	among	behind	down	into	on	toward	upon
after	around	beneath	for	near	over	under	with

- A **prepositional phrase** is a group of words that begins with a preposition and ends with a noun or pronoun.

  EXAMPLE: We borrowed the lawn mower **from Ken**.

- The noun or pronoun in the prepositional phrase is called the **object of the preposition**.

  EXAMPLE: Megan hurried **down** the **stairs**.

 Underline each prepositional phrase. Then circle each preposition.

1. Salt Lake City, Utah's capital and largest city, was founded in 1847.

2. Janice and Carla spent the day at the mall.

3. Standard time was adopted in the United States in 1884.

4. The geographic center of the United States is in Kansas.

5. The first safety lamp for miners was invented by Sir Humphrey Davy in 1816.

6. Many people of North Borneo live in houses that have been built on stilts in the Brunei River.

7. The children were charmed by the magician's tricks.

8. We visited the Royal Ontario Museum in Canada.

9. The first automobile show was held in New York City in 1900.

10. Self-government in the United States began in Jamestown in 1619.

11. The first street railway in the world was built in New York in 1832.

12. The inventor of the telephone was born in Scotland.

13. Who is the inventor of the printing press?

14. The shadowy outline of the giant skyscrapers loomed before us.

15. Our small boat bobbed in the waves.

16. The swivel chair was invented by Thomas Jefferson.

17. A raging storm fell upon the quiet valley.

18. I was lulled into sleep by the patter of the rain.

19. We found acorns beneath the tree.

20. That cow is standing in the middle of the road.

21. The child ran across the yard and around the tree.

22. A pine tree fell across the brook.

Prepositions and Prepositional Phrases, p. 2

 Underline each prepositional phrase. Then circle each preposition.

23. The first census of our country was taken in 1790.

24. Tons of violets are made into perfume each year.

25. The heart of a person pumps more than four quarts of blood in one minute.

26. The United States Patent Office was established in 1836.

27. One of the secrets of success is the wise use of leisure time.

28. The school board held its annual banquet at this hotel.

29. Duke Ellington was born in Washington, D.C.

30. Deposits of iron ore exist near the western end of the Great Lakes.

31. The bridge across this stream was destroyed by the recent storm.

32. Many herds of cattle once grazed on these plains.

33. The huddle in football was first used by a team from Georgia University in 1896.

34. The first skyscraper was built in Chicago.

35. Travelers of a century ago journeyed by stagecoach.

36. The huge tower of stone in Delhi in India is a monument to the skill of its builders.

37. The quiet of the evening was broken by the rumbling of thunder.

38. The parachutist was injured when her parachute caught in a tree.

39. Aviation was born on a sand dune in North Carolina in 1903.

40. The first trolley car was installed in Richmond in 1885.

41. A box of rusty nails was in the corner of the garage.

42. Don't stand near the edge of that steep cliff.

43. The ground was covered with a deep snow.

44. Twenty cars were involved in the accident on the expressway.

45. The study of geography teaches us about the features of other lands.

46. A thin column of smoke rose from the chimney of the cabin.

47. In the distance, we saw the top of the snowcapped peak.

48. Place the book upon the shelf.

49. At one time, Philadelphia was the capital of the United States.

50. The football sailed between the goal posts.

51. The report of the secretary was given at the beginning of the meeting.

52. A group of cheering fans waited at the entrance.

53. The hot-air balloon drifted toward the ground.

54. Let's have our picnic beneath this huge tree.

55. In the glow of the fading light, we drove along the road.

56. Emily lives near the new mall.

57. Look in the catalog to see if this book is in the library.

58. The tour guide led us through the halls of the mansion.

59. The theater group is meeting to discuss its productions for next year.

Conjunctions

> - A **conjunction** is a word used to join words or groups of words.
>   EXAMPLE: Jenna **and** her sister are in Arizona.
> - These are some commonly used conjunctions:
>
> | | | | | | | |
> |---|---|---|---|---|---|---|
> | although | because | however | or | that | when | while |
> | and | but | if | since | though | whereas | yet |
> | as | for | nor | than | unless | whether | |
>
> - Some conjunctions are used in pairs. These include either . . . or, neither . . . nor, both . . . and, and not only . . . but also.

 Underline each conjunction.

1. He and I are friends.
2. Darrell likes tennis, whereas Cedric prefers running.
3. We had to wait since it was raining.
4. We left early, but we missed the train.
5. The show was not only long but also boring.
6. Neither the chairs nor the tables had been dusted.
7. Hail and sleet fell during the storm.
8. Neither Carmen nor Kara was able to attend the meeting.
9. I have neither time nor energy to waste.
10. Bowling and tennis are my favorite sports.
11. Either Dan or Don will bring a portable radio.
12. The people in the car and the people in the van exchanged greetings.
13. Neither cookies nor cake is on your diet.
14. Although I like to take photographs, I am not a good photographer.
15. Did you see Wilson when he visited here?
16. We are packing our bags since our vacation trip begins tomorrow.
17. She cannot concentrate while you are making so much noise.
18. Unless you hurry, the party will be over before you arrive.
19. We enjoyed the visit although we were very tired.
20. Both mammals and birds are warm-blooded.
21. She is one performer who can both sing and dance.
22. Unless you have some objections, I will submit this report.
23. Neither dogs nor cats are allowed in this park.
24. April watered the plants while Luis mowed the lawn.
25. I will see you when you are feeling better.
26. Either Ms. Andretti or Ms. Garcia will teach that course.
27. We got here late because we lost our directions.

Language: Usage and Practice 8, SV 1419027859

Double Negatives

> • Do not use <u>not</u> with the adverbs <u>never</u>, <u>hardly</u>, <u>scarcely</u>, <u>seldom</u>, <u>none</u>, and <u>nothing</u>.
> • One clause cannot properly contain two negatives.
>   EXAMPLES:
>   There wasn't anything left in the refrigerator. (Correct)
>   There wasn't nothing left in the refrigerator. (Incorrect)

 Underline the correct word in parentheses to complete each sentence.

1. We couldn't see (anything, nothing) through the fog.

2. The suspect wouldn't admit (anything, nothing).

3. I don't know (any, none) of the people on this bus.

4. Rosa couldn't do (anything, nothing) about changing the time of our program.

5. We didn't have (any, no) printed programs.

6. I don't want (any, no) cereal for breakfast this morning.

7. You must not speak to (anyone, no one) about our surprise party plans.

8. There isn't (any, no) ink in this pen.

9. Didn't you make (any, no) copies for the other people?

10. I haven't had (any, no) time to repair the lawn mower.

11. She hasn't said (anything, nothing) about her accident.

12. Hardly (anything, nothing) pleases him.

13. There aren't (any, no) pears in this supermarket.

14. There isn't (any, no) newspaper in that little town.

15. There wasn't (anybody, nobody) in the house.

16. Please don't ask him (any, no) questions.

17. I haven't solved (any, none) of my problems.

18. I haven't done (anything, nothing) to offend Greg.

19. We don't have (any, no) water pressure.

20. Our team wasn't (any, no) match for the opposing team.

21. I couldn't hear (anything, nothing) because of the airplane's noise.

22. The salesperson didn't have (any, no) samples on display.

23. I haven't (any, no) money with me.

24. Hasn't he cooked (any, none) of the pasta?

25. We haven't (any, no) more packages to wrap.

26. Wasn't there (anyone, no one) at home?

27. My dog has never harmed (anybody, nobody).

28. They seldom have (anyone, no one) absent from their meetings.

29. There weren't (any, no) clouds in the sky.

Language: Usage and Practice 8, SV 1419027859

Unit 3 Test

Darken the circle by the term that describes the noun.

1. scissors (A) abstract (B) concrete (C) collective   4. pride   (A) abstract (B) concrete (C) collective

2. team   (A) abstract (B) concrete (C) collective   5. wastebasket (A) abstract (B) concrete (C) collective

3. fruit   (A) abstract (B) concrete (C) collective   6. happiness   (A) abstract (B) concrete (C) collective

Darken the circle by the term that describes the noun.

7. Jason's (A) singular (B) plural (C) possessive   10. woman's (A) singular (B) plural (C) possessive

8. flies   (A) singular (B) plural (C) possessive   11. pumpkin (A) singular (B) plural (C) possessive

9. geese   (A) singular (B) plural (C) possessive   12. ribbon   (A) singular (B) plural (C) possessive

Darken the circle by the sentence in which the appositive is underlined.

13. (A) Her oldest daughter, Emma, won the debate.

    (B) Bill serves as a volunteer firefighter, in addition to being a reporter.

    (C) "Why," asked Marcy, "did you pretend to be gone?"

    (D) Mayor Shea, our new mayor, has spent years in public service.

Darken the circle by the sentence in which the antecedent is underlined.

14. (A) Every contestant did his or her best.

    (B) The planets revolve around the sun in their orbits.

    (C) Most of the employees have taken their vacations.

    (D) George finished his work early and went to the lake.

Darken the circle by the term that describes the underlined word or words.

15. Jeff wants to go after school.   (A) infinitive (B) gerund (C) participle

16. The bubbling brook was a beautiful sight.   (A) infinitive (B) gerund (C) participle

17. Helping others is very rewarding.   (A) infinitive (B) gerund (C) participle

18. Don't forget to write to me while you're away. (A) infinitive (B) gerund (C) participle

19. Baked pumpkin seeds are delicious.   (A) infinitive (B) gerund (C) participle

20. Dan's hobby is building model airplanes.   (A) infinitive (B) gerund (C) participle

Language: Usage and Practice 8, SV 1419027859

Unit 3 Test, p. 2

Darken the circle by the correct verb to complete each sentence.

21. I had _____ to see the new baby.   (A) came   (B) coming   (C) come

22. Marie _____ blood at the health center.   (A) gave   (B) given   (C) give

23. Luis is _____ some vegetables in his garden.   (A) grew   (B) grown   (C) growing

24. My brother has _____ a military jet.   (A) flown   (B) flying   (C) flew

25. They are _____ in the race today.   (A) swimming   (B) swam   (C) swim

26. Jason _____ his winter coat to the game.   (A) wore   (B) worn   (C) wearing

27. He has _____ awake for hours.   (A) laid   (B) lain   (C) layed

28. Please _____ me to sew.   (A) teach   (B) learn   (C) teaching

29. It is _____ to get cloudy.   (A) begin   (B) beginning   (C) began

30. Did you _____ that iced tea?   (A) drank   (B) drunk   (C) drink

31. Just _____ the books there.   (A) lie   (B) lay   (C) laid

32. I'll _____ here to rest.   (A) set   (B) sit   (C) sat

Darken the circle by the sentence in which pronouns are used correctly.

33. (A) We hoped the winning contestant was her.
    (B) The woman for whom we gave the party was delighted.
    (C) The dog licked it's paw after stepping on the thistle.
    (D) He went to the store with Hoan and I.

34. (A) The elephant uses its trunk to drink water.
    (B) William and Todd played them guitars.
    (C) Janice and me chose the same restaurant.
    (D) He said it was them who took it.

35. (A) Whom broke this vase?
    (B) The new house is their.
    (C) Elena and she tied for first place.
    (D) It couldn't have been them.

36. (A) Did him answer the phone?
    (B) Between you and I, I think it's wrong.
    (C) Dirk is me younger brother.
    (D) Whom did you ask first?

Darken the circle by the correct adjective or adverb to complete each sentence.

37. This book is the _____ I have ever read.   (A) more interesting   (B) most interesting   (C) interesting

38. I can run _____ in my new shoes.   (A) more quick   (B) more quicker   (C) more quickly

39. Where did you find _____ shoes?   (A) them   (B) those   (C) that

Darken the circle by the sentence that has the prepositional phrase underlined.

40. (A) I didn't want to trust her at the beginning.
    (B) The house on the hill was completely destroyed by fire.
    (C) In the early evening, the moon came out.
    (D) Throw down the blanket, please.

Using Capital Letters

> • Capitalize the first word of a sentence and of each line of poetry.
>   EXAMPLES: Maria wrote a poem. It began as follows:
>   One cold, starry night
>   We saw the stars taking flight.
> • Capitalize all proper nouns.
>   EXAMPLES: Ellen Kennan, Uncle John, First Street, Spain, Virginia,
>   White Mountains, New Year's Day, March, Miles High School,
>   *Sea Voyager*
> • Capitalize all proper adjectives. A proper adjective is an adjective that is made
>   from a proper noun.
>   EXAMPLES: the French language, German food, American tourists
> • Capitalize the first word of a quotation.
>   EXAMPLE: Tonya said, "Everyone should learn a poem."
> • Capitalize the first, last, and all important words in the titles of books, poems,
>   stories, and songs.
>   EXAMPLES: "The Necklace"; *The Call of the Wild*

 Circle each letter that should be capitalized. Write the capital letter above it.

1. henry wadsworth longfellow wove the history of america into his poems "evangeline"

   and "the courtship of miles standish."

2. "the midnight ride of paul revere" is another of longfellow's poems.

3. The british ship *titanic* sank on its first trip from england to the united states.

4. the first law course offered by an american college was taught by george wythe.

5. he taught many famous people, including thomas jefferson and james monroe.

6. The mississippi river flows through vicksburg, mississippi, and new orleans, louisiana.

7. "what time do the church bells ring?" asked amelia.

8. robert answered, "i believe they ring every half hour."

9. Many centuries ago, vikings lived in what is now known as norway, sweden, and denmark.

10. the song "the battle hymn of the republic" was written by julia ward howe.

11. Mr. james nelson lives in chicago, illinois.

12. he asked, "have you ever seen a waterfall?"

13. The president of the united states lives in the white house.

14. Last summer I visited a hopi reservation.

15. sequoia national park is on the western slope of the sierra nevada mountains in California.

Using Capital Letters, p. 2

> • Capitalize a person's title when it comes before a name.
>   EXAMPLES: Doctor Lemer, Judge Kennedy, Governor Thompson
> • Capitalize abbreviations of titles.
>   EXAMPLES: Mr. J. D. Little, Dr. Simon, Pres. Truman

 Circle each letter that should be capitalized. Write the capital letter above it.

16. mayor jones and senator small attended the awards banquet Friday night.

17. dr. fox is a veterinarian at the local animal hospital.

18. The invitation said to respond to ms. hilary johnson.

19. No one expected judge randall to rule in favor of the defendant.

20. We were disappointed that gov. dickson couldn't speak at graduation.

21. In his place will be senator christopher larson.

22. The speaker will be introduced by supt. adams.

23. Will miss alden be the new history instructor?

24. dr. tabor is a surgeon at Parkside Hospital.

25. His first patient was mr. william benton.

> • Capitalize abbreviations of days and months, parts of addresses, and titles of members of the armed forces.
> • Also capitalize all letters in the abbreviations of states.
>   EXAMPLES: Fri.; Aug.; 267 N. Concord Ave.; Col. Fernando Gonzales;
>   Hartford, CT

 Circle each letter that should be capitalized. Write the capital letter above it.

26. When is maj. hanson expected back from his trip overseas?

27. The garage sale is at 101 w. charles st.

28. Have you ever been to orlando, fl?

29. There is a house for sale at the corner of maple ave. and sunset st.

30. Everyone in our company has the first mon. off in sept. for Labor Day.

31. The highest award for service was given to gen. t. j. quint.

32. The letter from memphis, tn, took only two days to arrive.

33. Did you know that col. kravitz will be stationed in dover, nh?

34. His address will be 1611 falmouth harbor, dover, nh 03805.

Language: Usage and Practice 8, SV 1419027859

Using End Punctuation

> - Use a **period** at the end of a declarative sentence.
>   EXAMPLE: We are going to Mexico on our vacation.
> - Use a **question mark** at the end of an interrogative sentence.
>   EXAMPLE: Do you know whose picture is on the one-dollar bill?

 Use a period or question mark to end each sentence below.

1. Does this road wind uphill all the way to Roderick's house____
2. Los Angeles, Mexico City, and Rome have all been sites of the Olympic Games____
3. Were there really one hundred people standing in line at the theater____
4. Wisconsin raises hay, corn, and oats____
5. Pablo, Tom, Carlos, and Ling were nominated as candidates____
6. Whom did you see, Elizabeth____
7. Haydn, Mozart, Mendelssohn, and Beethoven composed symphonies____
8. Hummingbirds and barn swallows migrate____
9. Do you think that Napoleon was an able leader____
10. Does Louisa live in Los Angeles, California____
11. Who wrote the Declaration of Independence____
12. We flew from Seattle, Washington, to Miami, Florida____
13. Roy Avery is a guest of Mr. and Mrs. Benson____
14. Anna, have you read "The Gift of the Magi" by O. Henry____

 Add the correct end punctuation where needed in the paragraphs below.

Have you ever heard of Harriet Tubman and the Underground Railroad____ During the Civil War in the United States, Harriet Tubman, a former slave, helped more than three hundred slaves escape to freedom____ Tubman led slaves on the dangerous route of the Underground Railroad____ It was not actually a railroad but a series of secret homes and shelters that led through the South to the free North and Canada____ How dangerous was her work____ There were large rewards offered by slaveholders for her capture____ But Tubman was never caught____ She said proudly, "I never lost a passenger____" She was called the Moses of her people____

During the war, she worked as a spy for the Union army____ An excellent guide, she would lead soldiers into enemy camps____ She also served as a nurse and cook for the soldiers____ She was well respected among leading abolitionists of the time____ She was also a strong supporter of women's rights____

Do you know what she did after the war____ She settled in Auburn, New York, and took care of her parents and any other needy black person____ She was always low on money but never refused anyone____ Later, she set up a home for poor African Americans____

Using End Punctuation, p. 2

- Use a **period** at the end of an imperative sentence.
  EXAMPLE: Please answer the telephone.
- Use an **exclamation point** at the end of an exclamatory sentence and after an interjection that shows strong feeling.
- If a command expresses great excitement, use an exclamation point at the end of the sentence.
  EXAMPLES: Ouch!   Follow that car!   The ringing is so loud!   My ears hurt!

 Add periods or exclamation points where needed in the sentences below.

15. I love to hike in the mountains____
16. Just look at the view in the distance____
17. Be sure to wear the right kind of shoes____
18. Ouch____ My blister is killing me____
19. Talk quietly and walk softly____
20. Don't scare away the wildlife____
21. Look____ It's a bald eagle____
22. I can't believe how big it is____
23. Take a picture before it flies away____
24. Its wings are bigger than I had ever imagined____
25. It's one of the most breathtaking sights I've ever seen____
26. Oh, look this way____ Here comes another one____
27. This is the luckiest day of my life____
28. Sit down on that tree stump____
29. Pick another place to sit____

 Add the correct end punctuation where needed in the paragraphs below.

Do you find cats fascinating____ If you answered yes, you share the same opinion that many people have had for centuries____ About 5,000 years ago in Egypt, cats became accepted household pets____ That was a long time ago____ Cats were actually worshipped in ancient Egypt____

The different members of the cat family have certain things in common____ House cats and wild cats all walk on the tips of their toes____ Isn't that incredible____ Even though no cats like water, they can all swim____ Another thing that all cats have in common is a keen hunting ability____ Part of this is due to their eyesight____ They see well at night and in dim light____ Did you know that the cat is the only animal that purrs____ A cat uses its whiskers to feel____ Its sense of touch is located in its whiskers____ The coat of a cat can be long-haired or short-haired, solid-colored, or striped____ Some cats even have spots____ Can you name any types of cats____

Name _____ Date _____   Date _____

Using Commas

- Use a **comma** between words or groups of words that are in a series.
  - EXAMPLE: Colorado, Canadian, Ohio, Mississippi, and Missouri are names of well-known American rivers.
- Use a comma before a conjunction in a compound sentence.
  - EXAMPLE: Once the rivers were used mainly for transportation, but today they are used for recreation and industry.
- Use a comma after a subordinate clause when it begins a sentence.
  - EXAMPLE: When I got to the theater, the movie had already begun.

 Add commas where needed in the sentences below.

1. Anita Travis and Nick went to the tennis tournament.
2. Before they found their seats the first match had already begun.
3. It was a close game and they weren't disappointed by the final score.
4. They had come to cheer for Antonio Fergas and he was the winner.
5. Although his opponent was very good Fergas never missed returning a serve.
6. While they watched the match Anita clapped cheered and kept score.
7. Travis and Nick watched a number of different matches but Anita followed Fergas.
8. He was signing autographs and Anita was first in line.
9. Antonio asked her name signed a tennis ball and shook her hand.
10. Because they enjoyed the match so much Travis Nick and Anita made plans to come back for the final match the next day.
11. They planned to see the men's women's and doubles' finals.
12. Fergas won the entire tournament and he became the youngest champion in the history of the tournament.

- Use a comma to set off a quotation from the rest of the sentence.
  - EXAMPLES: "We'd better leave early," said Travis.
    - Travis said, "We'd better leave early."
- Use two commas to set off a divided quotation. Do not capitalize the first word of the second part of the quotation.
  - EXAMPLE: "We'd better leave," Travis said, "or we'll be stuck in traffic."

 Add commas to the quotations below.

13. "The first match starts at 9:00 A.M." said Travis.
14. Anita asked "Do you want to get seats in the same section as yesterday?"
15. "That's fine with me" said Nick.
16. Nick said "Fergas's first match is in Court B."
17. "I'll bring the binoculars" said Anita "and you can bring the cooler."

www.harcourtschoolsupply.com
© Harcourt Achieve Inc. All rights reserved.   **86**   **Unit 4: Capitalization and Punctuation**
Language: Usage and Practice 8, SV 1419027859

Using Commas, p. 2

> • Use a comma to set off the name of a person who is being addressed.
>   EXAMPLE: Phil, would you like to leave now?
> • Use a comma to set off words like <u>yes</u>, <u>no</u>, <u>well</u>, <u>oh</u>, <u>first</u>, <u>next</u>, and <u>finally</u> at the beginning of a sentence.
>   EXAMPLE: Well, I guess so.
> • Use a comma to set off an appositive.
>   EXAMPLE: Alvin, Phil's brother, is a dentist in Pittsburgh.

 Add commas where needed in the sentences below.

18. Dr. Perillo a nutritionist is an expert on proper eating.

19. "Students it's important to eat a well-balanced diet," she said.

20. "Yes but how do we know what the right foods are?" asked one student.

21. "First you need to look carefully at your eating habits," said Dr. Perillo.

22. "Yes you should keep a journal of the foods you eat," she said.

23. "Dr. Perillo what do you mean by the right servings?" asked Emilio.

24. "OK good question," she said.

25. "A serving Emilio is a certain amount of a food," said Dr. Perillo.

26. "Dave a cross-country runner will need more calories than a less active student," explained Dr. Perillo.

27. "Class remember to eat foods from the five basic food groups," she said.

 Add commas where needed in the paragraphs below.

Our neighbor Lamont has fruit trees on his property. "Lamont what kinds of fruit do you grow?" I asked. "Well I grow peaches apricots pears and plums" he replied. "Wow! That's quite a variety" I said. Lamont's son Riley helps his dad care for the trees. "Oh it's constant work and care" Riley said "but the delicious results are worth the effort." After the fruit is harvested Riley's mother Charlotte cans the fruit for use throughout the year. She makes preserves and she gives them as gifts for special occasions. Charlotte sells some of her preserves to Kurt Simmons the owner of a local shop. People come from all over the county to buy Charlotte's preserves.

Riley's aunt Fay grows corn tomatoes beans and squash in her garden. Each year she selects her best vegetables and enters them in the fair. She has won blue ribbons medals and certificates for her vegetables. "Oh I just like being outside. That's why I enjoy gardening" Fay said. Fay's specialty squash-and-tomato bread is one of the most delicious breads I have ever tasted.

Language: Usage and Practice 8, SV 1419027859

Using Quotation Marks and Apostrophes

- Use **quotation marks** to show the exact words of a speaker.
- Use a comma or another punctuation mark to separate the quotation from the rest of the sentence.
- A quotation may be placed at the beginning or at the end of a sentence.
- Begin the quote with a capital letter.
- Be sure to include all the speaker's words within the quotation marks.
  EXAMPLES: "Let's go to the movie," said Sharona.
  "What time," asked Marcus, "does the movie begin?"

 Add quotation marks and other punctuation where needed in the sentences below.

1. Mary, do you think this is Christine's pen asked Luci.

2. Luci said I don't know. It looks like the kind she uses.

3. Well, I think it's out of ink, Mary replied.

4. Have you seen Barton's car? asked Angelina.

5. No said Celia, I haven't gotten over to his apartment this week.

6. Angelina said It's really pretty. I can't wait to ride in it.

7. I can't believe how late it is exclaimed Hector.

8. Carmelo asked Where are you going on vacation this summer?

9. My brother and I are visiting our parents in Maine said Bradley.

10. Tell me, Ming said how many cats you have.

11. Alison said The last time we counted, there were four.

12. Will you be taking the bus home asked Jason or do you need a ride?

- Use an **apostrophe** in a contraction to show where a letter or letters have been taken out.
  EXAMPLE: **Let's** go to the store.   I **can't** go until tomorrow.
- Use an apostrophe to form a possessive noun. Add 's to most singular nouns. Add ' to most plural nouns. Add 's to a few nouns that have irregular plurals.
  EXAMPLES: **Maria's** sons are musicians.   The **sons'** voices are magnificent.
  They sing in a **children's** choir.

 Write the words in which an apostrophe has been left out. Insert apostrophes where they are needed.

13. Im sorry I cant make it to the concert. _____

14. I cant go until Taylors project is completed. _____

15. Ill need two nights notice. _____

16. Ive heard that the bandleaders favorite piece will be played last. _____

17. Isnt it one of Cole Porters songs? _____

Language: Usage and Practice 8, SV 1419027859

Using Colons and Semicolons

> - Use a **colon** after the greeting in a business letter.
>   EXAMPLES: Dear Mrs. Miller: Dear Sirs:
> - Use a colon between the hour and the minutes when writing the time.
>   EXAMPLES: 11:45   3:30   9:10
> - Use a colon to introduce a list.
>   EXAMPLE: The shopping cart contained the following items: milk, eggs, crackers, apples, soap, and paper towels.

 Add colons where needed in the sentences below.

1. At 9 1 0 this morning, we'll be leaving for the natural history museum.

2. Please bring the following materials with you pencils, paper, erasers, and a notebook.

3. The bus will be back at 4 0 0 to pick us up.

4. The special exhibit on birds contains the following types prehistoric birds, seabirds, and domestic birds.

5. The letter we wrote to the museum began "Dear Sir Please let us know when the special exhibition on penguins will be shown at your museum."

6. He told us that we could find out more about the following kinds of penguins the Emperor, the Adelie, and the Magellan.

7. We were afraid there would be so much to see that we wouldn't be ready to leave at 3 3 0 when the museum closed.

> - Use a **semicolon** between the clauses of a compound sentence that are closely related but not connected by a conjunction.
> - Do not capitalize the word after a semicolon.
>   EXAMPLE: Hummingbirds and barn swallows migrate; some kinds of birds live in one place all year.

 Rewrite each sentence below, adding semicolons where needed.

8. Colleen is a clever teacher she is also an inspiring one.

_____

9. Her lectures are interesting they are full of information.

_____

10. She has a college degree in history world history is her specialty.

_____

11. She begins her classes by answering questions she ends them by asking questions.

_____

Name _____ Date _____

Using Other Punctuation

> - Use a **hyphen** between the parts of some compound words.
>   EXAMPLES: poverty-stricken   sixty-three   part-time
>   able-bodied   brother-in-law   hard-boiled
> - Use a hyphen to separate the syllables of a word that is carried over from one line to the next.
>   EXAMPLE: So many things were going on at once that no one could pos-sibly guess how the play would end.

 Add hyphens where needed in these sentences.

1. The director told us that there would be room for only two busloads, or eighty four people.

2. The play was going to be in an old fashioned theater.

3. Between acts the theater was completely dark, but the orchestra con tinued to play anyway.

4. The vice president was played by Luke Lowe.

> - Use a **dash** to set off words that interrupt the main thought of a sentence or to show a sudden change of thought.
>   EXAMPLES: We were surprised—even shocked—by the news.
>   It was Wednesday—no, it was Friday—that I was sick.

 Add dashes where needed in the sentences below.

5. There was a loud boom what a fright from the back of the theater.

6. We all turned around I even jumped up to see what it was.

7. It was part of the play imagine that meant to add suspense.

8. I'd love to see the play again maybe next week and bring Andrea.

> - Underline or italicize the titles of books, plays, magazines, films, and television series.
>   EXAMPLE: We read <u>Romeo and Juliet</u> last term.
> - Underline or italicize foreign words and phrases.
>   EXAMPLE: "*Adieu*," said the French actor to his co-star.

 In the sentences below, underline where needed.

9. We saw the movie Of Mice and Men after we had read the novel.

10. In Spanish, Hasta la vista means "See you later."

11. My favorite book is Little Women.

12. I took a copy of Time magazine out of the library.

Language: Usage and Practice 8, SV 1419027859

Unit 4 Test

Darken the circle by the word in each sentence that should be capitalized.

1. Was senator Curtis a member of the foreign delegation?

   Ⓐ senator Ⓑ member Ⓒ foreign Ⓓ delegation

2. The foreign students enjoyed the mexican food.

   Ⓐ foreign Ⓑ students Ⓒ mexican Ⓓ food

3. Their principal was the author of a book called Getting to know Your Students.

   Ⓐ principal Ⓑ author Ⓒ to Ⓓ know

4. My uncle has a cabin near detroit, Michigan, by the lake.

   Ⓐ uncle Ⓑ cabin Ⓒ detroit Ⓓ lake

5. where did the three men and their fathers go on vacation?

   Ⓐ where Ⓑ men Ⓒ fathers Ⓓ vacation

6. "I will just be a moment," said Kate. "please wait for me."

   Ⓐ moment Ⓑ said Ⓒ please Ⓓ me

7. The speaker told the audience at Howell auditorium that he was an expert.

   Ⓐ speaker Ⓑ audience Ⓒ auditorium Ⓓ expert

8. My mother's sister moved to the city and lives at 947 west Woodpecker Way.

   Ⓐ mother's Ⓑ sister Ⓒ city Ⓓ west

Darken the circle by the sentence in which capitalization is used correctly.

9. Ⓐ The nine planets of our solar system revolve around the sun in elliptical orbits.

   Ⓑ Jeremy said, "let's go to the exhibit at the Museum of Natural History."

   Ⓒ I need to go to the library and check out how to Refinish Furniture the Easy Way.

   Ⓓ Captain Hensley moved his family to White Air Force base.

Darken the circle by the sentence in which end punctuation is used correctly.

10. Ⓐ I told you the truth?

    Ⓑ He went back to the house!

    Ⓒ What a fantastic idea!

    Ⓓ Don't be sad?

11. Ⓐ I like to read when the weather is bad?

    Ⓑ We almost made it on time?

    Ⓒ Can we help you?

    Ⓓ Haven't I met you before!

12. Ⓐ Look. There's a rainbow.

    Ⓑ Snakebites can be dangerous.

    Ⓒ I'd like to know her name?

    Ⓓ When will you leave for the lake.

13. Ⓐ Ouch. I burned myself.

    Ⓑ That's her favorite dessert?

    Ⓒ Everyone likes ice cream?

    Ⓓ Take the first exit.

Unit 4 Test, p. 2

Darken the circle by the sentence in which commas are used correctly.

14. Ⓐ I like apples but, Dudley doesn't.
    Ⓑ We have a cat, a dog and a fish at home.
    Ⓒ How, are you Frank?
    Ⓓ Renee said, "Yes, I can go!"

15. Ⓐ After calling her, did you see Amy?
    Ⓑ Karina please come, or I'll miss you.
    Ⓒ My neighbor Mr. Ramos said, "Yes, Jim."
    Ⓓ They elected Chea, Neena and Jesse.

16. Ⓐ Before school I saw Suzi, Neil and, Dan.
    Ⓑ "What a surprise, Kayla!" shouted Gina.
    Ⓒ Ashton do you like peas, or carrots better?
    Ⓓ I almost, forgot Miguel!

17. Ⓐ "That's a pretty sweater, Lin" said Selina.
    Ⓑ When we arrive they'll recognize us, Matt.
    Ⓒ Patrice, my cousin, would like to come.
    Ⓓ Of course I'd love to see you Justin.

Darken the circle by the sentence in which quotation marks are used correctly.

18. Ⓐ "Can you come? Tom said."
    Ⓑ Carlos asked, "Did you see the show?
    Ⓒ "Yes, I will," answered Jana.
    Ⓓ "Robyn told us, "Don't step there!

19. Ⓐ "I'd like to go, said Lin."
    Ⓑ Franci said, "Please" hold this.
    Ⓒ "Are you Canadian? asked June.
    Ⓓ Jeff said, "I can't believe it!"

Darken the circle by the sentence in which apostrophes are used correctly.

20. Ⓐ Don't leave me here alone.
    Ⓑ He has'nt arrived yet.
    Ⓒ That notebook is her's.
    Ⓓ Forget whats' been said already.

21. Ⓐ The teacher is'nt here yet.
    Ⓑ Their's is the one on the far left.
    Ⓒ Voting is every person's right.
    Ⓓ Shell be back soon with the paper.

Darken the circle by the sentence in which colons or semicolons are used correctly.

22. Ⓐ Will Renee be there by: 730?
    Ⓑ The time is now 1:20.
    Ⓒ Do you have these items a pencil: and paper?
    Ⓓ By 200; please be at the station.

23. Ⓐ Please: make a list.
    Ⓑ We like to visit; museums in Chicago.
    Ⓒ It was 2:00: but nobody showed up.
    Ⓓ He's my brother; I'm his sister.

Darken the circle by the sentence in which dashes or hyphens are used correctly.

24. Ⓐ Do you like hard boiled-eggs?
    Ⓑ Tell me—I'm starting it now—how to do this project.
    Ⓒ I am working-on a short term basis.
    Ⓓ All thirty one-people looked bored.

25. Ⓐ We like to visit the wonderful muse-ums in Chicago, Illinois.
    Ⓑ There are twenty seven-people in my pottery class.
    Ⓒ My grand-mother is ninety two years old.
    Ⓓ Jacey made a pineapple upside down-cake.

Darken the circle by the sentence in which underlining is used correctly.

26. Ⓐ Entertainment Weekly is fun to read.
    Ⓑ She is the author of The Way It Was Then.
    Ⓒ "Por favor," said Enrique.
    Ⓓ Xena is her favorite TV series.

27. Ⓐ I saw the play Jane Eyre four times.
    Ⓑ Do you read the Wall Street Journal?
    Ⓒ I checked that fact in World Book Encyclopedia.
    Ⓓ Have you read the book Huckleberry Finn?

Writing Sentences

> * Every **sentence** has a base consisting of a simple subject and a simple predicate.
>   - EXAMPLE: People applied.
> * Expand the meaning of a sentence by adding adjectives, adverbs, and prepositional phrases to the sentence base.
>   - EXAMPLE: **Several** people applied **at the technical institute last week.**

 Expand the meaning of each sentence base below by adding adjectives, adverbs, and prepositional phrases. Write your expanded sentence.

1. (Visitors toured.) _____

2. (Machines roared.) _____

3. (People lifted.) _____

4. (Work stopped.) _____

5. (Buzzer sounded.) _____

 Imagine two different scenes for each sentence base below. Write an expanded sentence to describe each scene you imagine.

6. (Day began.)   **a.** _____

     b. _____

7. (Workers operated.)   **a.** _____

     b. _____

8. (Supervisor explained.)   **a.** _____

     b. _____

9. (Shipment arrived.)   **a.** _____

     b. _____

10. (People unpacked.)   **a.** _____

     b. _____

11. (Automobiles appeared.)   **a.** _____

     b. _____

12. (Friend cooked.)   **a.** _____

     b. _____

Language: Usage and Practice 8, SV 1419027859

Name _____ Date _____

Writing Paragraphs

> • A **paragraph** is a group of sentences about one **main idea**. All the sentences in a paragraph relate to the main idea.
> • The first sentence in a paragraph is always indented.
>   EXAMPLE: People work for a variety of reasons. One of the most important reasons people work is to earn money to buy goods and services they need. Work can also provide enjoyment or lead to achieving personal goals.

 In each paragraph below, cross out the sentence that is not related to the main idea of the paragraph. Then write a new sentence that is related.

1.   Bob and Terrence have been friends since the day Bob's family first moved into the neighborhood. The boys were in the same class in both kindergarten and first grade. A few years later, they joined Scouts and worked together to earn merit badges. Bob's dad is an experienced carpenter. In junior high school, Bob was a star pitcher, while Terrence led their team in batting.

_____

2.   Rita's first job was at the swimming pool. Because she was a good swimmer and had passed a lifesaving course, she was asked to demonstrate swimming strokes during swimming instruction. She was not old enough to be an instructor. Sometimes she got jobs babysitting for families with children in the swimming program.

_____

 Choose one of the topics below and write a paragraph of three or four sentences that are related to it.

   a. Your first job   **c.** The job you'd most like to have
   b. The job everyone wants   **d.** Jobs in your community

_____

_____

_____

_____

_____

_____

_____

_____

_____

_____

_____

Language: Usage and Practice 8, SV 1419027859

Name _____ Date _____

Writing Topic Sentences

> - The **topic sentence** states the main idea of a paragraph.
> - It is often placed at the beginning of a paragraph.
>   EXAMPLE: **Young people can learn various skills by working in a fast-food restaurant.** They can learn how to use machines to cook food in a uniform way, how to handle money, and how to work with customers and with other employees.

 Underline the topic sentence in each paragraph below.

1. Working in a fast-food restaurant is a good first job for young people. The hours are flexible. No previous experience is needed. The work is not hard.

2. A popular ice-cream parlor in our town hires young people. Some work serving customers. Some work making special desserts. Others do cleanup and light maintenance.

3. Computers are used in fast-food restaurants. The cash register has a computer that totals purchase prices and computes change. Ovens and deep fryers have computers that regulate cooking temperatures.

 Write a topic sentence for each group of related sentences.

4. Working may conflict with other activities. There may not be enough time for you to complete housework. You may miss out on having fun with friends.

   Topic Sentence: _____

5. Kate manages the kitchen, plans the menus, and orders all the food. Jesse supervises the dining room. Jesse's sister does the bookkeeping for the restaurant. On weekends, my brother and I help clear the tables.

   Topic Sentence: _____

6. The dining room was decorated with advertisements from the fifties. The band played only music from the fifties, and the waiters and waitresses all wore black slacks and bright pink bow ties.

   Topic Sentence: _____

 Write a topic sentence for one of the topics below.

7. **a.** the best restaurant I've ever gone to   **c.** the job of waiter
   b. restaurants in our town   **d.** the worst meal I've ever eaten

   _____

   _____

   _____

Name _____   Date _____

Writing Supporting Details

> • The idea expressed in a topic sentence can be developed with sentences containing **supporting details**.
> • Details can include facts, examples, and reasons.

 Circle the topic sentence and underline four supporting details in the paragraph below.

In almost every professional sport, there are far more applicants than available jobs. Consider professional football. Every season, several hundred players are selected by thirty-two NFL teams. Of those chosen, only about ten percent are actually signed by a professional team. Furthermore, this number shrinks each year because team owners want smaller and smaller teams.

Answer the following questions about the supporting details you underlined.

1. What is one supporting detail that is a fact?

_____

_____

_____

2. What is a supporting detail that is a reason?

_____

_____

Read each topic sentence below and write three supporting details for each.

3. People who want a career in sports could teach physical education.

_____

_____

_____

4. Professional sports teams employ people other than players.

_____

_____

_____

_____

Language: Usage and Practice 8, SV 1419027859

Name _____   Date _____

Topic and Audience

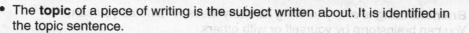

> • The **topic** of a piece of writing is the subject written about. It is identified in the topic sentence.
> • The **audience** is the person or persons who will read what is written.
>   EXAMPLES: parents, teenagers, school officials, engineers

✳ **Choose the most likely audience for each topic listed below. Write the letter of your choice on the line.**

a. parents   **c.** job counselors
b. high-school students   **d.** computer hobbyists

_____ 1. future of personal computers   _____ 3. jobs of the future

_____ 2. benefits of a college education   _____ 4. paying for college

✳ **Read the paragraph below and answer the questions that follow.**

    The evening was full of surprises. First, Lori forgot to tell me she had five children. I had seen only two of them at the store with her. She also forgot to mention the cats—to which I am violently allergic. Also, I wasn't prepared to fix the children dinner. I wrongly assumed that Lori would have fed them before I came. After getting everyone settled, I wondered if I should do the dishes. I figured that anyone with five children would appreciate having that job done.

5. What is the topic sentence? _____

6. Name two possible audiences for the paragraph.

_____

_____

7. Explain why each audience might be interested.

_____

_____

_____

_____

✳ **Choose two topics that interest you. Write a topic sentence for a paragraph about each topic. Then name an audience for each paragraph.**

8. Topic Sentence: _____

   Audience: _____

9. Topic Sentence: _____

   Audience: _____

Brainstorming

> - **Brainstorming** is a way to bring as many ideas to mind as you can.
> - You can brainstorm by yourself or with others.
> - As you brainstorm, write down your ideas. It is not necessary to write your ideas in sentence form.

Brainstorm about the things you would do if you were president of a major corporation. Write your ideas below.

1. _____

2. _____

3. _____

4. _____

Read the topics below. Choose one topic and circle it. Then brainstorm about its advantages and disadvantages. Write down as many ideas as you can.

a. volunteering   d. bicycle helmet laws

b. eating healthy food   e. automatic seat belts

c. mediating disagreements   f. self-defense training

5. _____

6. _____

7. _____

8. _____

9. _____

10. _____

Now write a brief paragraph about the topic you chose above that explains either the advantages or disadvantages of the topic.

_____

_____

_____

_____

_____

_____

Name _____ Date _____

Outlining

- Before you write, organize your thoughts by making an **outline**.
- An outline consists of the title of the topic, headings for the main ideas, and subheadings for the supporting details.
- Main headings are listed after Roman numerals. Subheadings are listed after capital letters. Details are listed after Arabic numerals.

EXAMPLE:

Topic	Should Young People Be Paid for Doing Chores?
Main heading	I. Benefits to parents
Subheadings	A. Chores get done
	B. More leisure time
Main heading	II. Benefits to young people
Subheading	A. Learn useful skills
Details	1. Clean and do laundry
	2. Budget time
Subheading	B. Become responsible

✳ **Choose a topic that interests you. Then write an outline for that topic, using the example outline as a guide.**

_____

_____

_____

_____

_____

_____

_____

_____

_____

_____

_____

_____

_____

_____

_____

Unit 5: Composition
Language: Usage and Practice 8, SV 1419027859

Persuasive Composition

> • The writer of a **persuasive composition** tries to convince others to accept a personal opinion.

 Read the following persuasive composition.

Everyone Should Learn to Use a Computer

Knowing how to use a computer is an essential skill for everyone who wants to succeed in today's world. One basic computer program that everyone should learn to use is the word processing program. Most types of writing are easily and professionally produced with a word processing program. For example, everyone must occasionally write a business letter. Using a computer allows you to arrange and rearrange information easily, making your writing clearer and more accurate. Word processing programs can help you check your spelling and grammar. A computer makes it easy to correct mistakes.

Computers can be used for much more than word processing, however. Other areas of interest and opportunity in the field of computers are graphic design, programming, and creating new games. Jobs in the computer field are growing, and strong computer skills can serve you well now and into the future.

 Answer the questions below.

1. List three facts the writer includes to persuade the reader.

_____

_____

_____

_____

_____

2. List two reasons the writer includes in the composition.

_____

_____

_____

3. List one example the writer uses to support the topic.

_____

_____

_____

Language: Usage and Practice 8, SV 1419027859

Persuasive Composition, p. 2

✳ **Choose one of the topic sentences below. Write a short paragraph in which you use facts to persuade your audience about the topic.**

4. The driver and front-seat passenger in a car face various consequences if they don't wear seat belts.

5. More people should carpool or use public transportation.

_____

_____

_____

_____

_____

✳ **Choose one of the topic sentences below. Write a short paragraph in which you use reasons to persuade your audience about the topic.**

6. Wearing seat belts ensures all passengers a safer ride.

7. The most important subject a person can learn about is _____.

_____

_____

_____

_____

_____

_____

✳ **Choose one of the topic sentences below. Write a short paragraph in which you use an example to persuade your audience about the topic.**

8. I know someone who wore a seat belt and survived a serious collision.

9. _____ make the best pets.

_____

_____

_____

_____

_____

_____

Language: Usage and Practice 8, SV 1419027859

Revising and Proofreading

- **Revising** gives you a chance to rethink and review what you have written and to improve your writing.
- Revise by adding words and information, by deleting unneeded words and information, and by moving words, sentences, and paragraphs around.
- **Proofreading** has to do with checking spelling, punctuation, grammar, and capitalization.
- Use proofreader's marks to show changes needed.

Proofreader's Marks

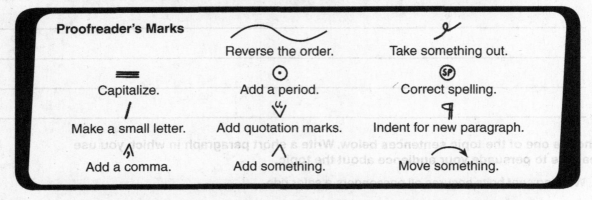

Reverse the order.

Take something out.

Capitalize.

Add a period.

Correct spelling.

Make a small letter.

Add quotation marks.

Indent for new paragraph.

Add a comma.

Add something.

Move something.

✱ **Rewrite the paragraph below. Correct the errors by following the proofreader's marks.**

¶ personal safety is one of the most important social issues today. Adults and children are worried about staying safe in all these places their homes, their schools, and the places they go to have fun. one of the best things a person can do is to act with confidence and awarness. Confidents means "believing," and awareness means seeing." Several studies have shone that people who act with confidence and awareness do not look like easy targets which is what criminals look for

_____

_____

_____

_____

_____

_____

_____

Language: Usage and Practice 8, SV 1419027859

Revising and Proofreading, p. 2

 Read the paragraphs below. Use proofreader's marks to revise and proofread the paragraphs. Then write your revised paragraphs below.

When your outside your home, your body Language is important very. if you straigt stand,

walk purposefully and pay attention to what is around you you will discourage Criminals

because you appear strong and alert. along with confidence and awareness Another tool

you can use all the time is your voice you can yell. Crimnals dont like to draw to attention

themselves and they don't like to be seen. Yelling may sometimes be embarrassing, but

your safety is more important than worrying about imbarrassment.

at home, its important to always keep your doors and windows locked you should never opent

the door to someone you don't know. You don't have to be polite to somebody who may be

trying to do you harm. This also applys to the telephone. If sombody you don't know calls

and tries to keep you engaged in a conservation, just hang up. you don't have to be polite to

somebody who is intruding in your life, especially if you don't know the person. always Keep

your safety in mind and act in a way that discourages criminals from bothering you

_____

_____

_____

_____

_____

_____

_____

_____

_____

_____

_____

_____

Language: Usage and Practice 8, SV 1419027859

Unit 5 Test

Read the paragraph. Then darken the circle by the correct answer to each question.

   As a singles tennis player, John McEnroe won the U.S. Open title on four occasions, and he won the prestigious Wimbledon championship three different times. McEnroe also won several major doubles tournaments after joining the professional tour in 1978. McEnroe was noted for his powerful serve-and-volley game, but it was his agility and quickness that sports fans admired most. Perhaps most important of all, McEnroe's tennis game had no weaknesses.

1. Which sentence could best be used as a topic sentence for the paragraph above?

   Ⓐ John McEnroe attempted a comeback in tennis.

   Ⓑ John McEnroe often had conflicts with officials during tennis matches.

   Ⓒ John McEnroe played tennis well on all court surfaces.

   Ⓓ John McEnroe was one of the most talented tennis players in the world.

2. Which sentence would add the most appropriate supporting detail to the paragraph above?

   Ⓐ McEnroe had a single-minded approach, which helped make him a champion.

   Ⓑ McEnroe was born in Wiesbaden, West Germany.

   Ⓒ McEnroe often beat Jimmy Connors.

   Ⓓ One of McEnroe's doubles partners was Peter Fleming.

3. Which audience would be the most interested in this paragraph?

   Ⓐ preschoolers   Ⓑ bus drivers   Ⓒ grandparents   Ⓓ athletes

4. What does the author use most to persuade readers to accept his or her opinion about John McEnroe?

   Ⓐ examples   Ⓑ facts   Ⓒ reasons   Ⓓ jokes

Darken the circle by the correct answer to each question.

5. Which would you use to bring as many ideas to mind as possible?

   Ⓐ outlining   Ⓑ brainstorming   Ⓒ persuading

6. Which would be an example of persuasive writing?

   Ⓐ letter to the editor   Ⓑ report   Ⓒ outline

7. What is the subject of a piece of writing called?

   Ⓐ example   Ⓑ detail   Ⓒ topic

8. Which is a group of sentences about one main idea?

   Ⓐ topic sentences   Ⓑ outline   Ⓒ paragraph

9. Which is not included in supporting details about a topic?

   Ⓐ outlines   Ⓑ facts   Ⓒ reasons

10. Which states the main idea of a paragraph?

   Ⓐ example   Ⓑ topic sentence   Ⓒ reason

Unit 5 Test, p. 2

Use the outline to answer the questions. Darken the circle by the correct answer.

Topic: Staying Fit and Healthy

   I. Food
      A. Eating right
      B. _____
         1. Vitamins
         2. Minerals
  II. _____
      A. Walking
      B. Running
      C. Other
         1. Weights
         2. Machines
  III. _____
      A. Mind/body
      B. Positive thinking

11. Which best fits on the line for II.?

  Ⓐ Attitude

  Ⓑ Exercise

  Ⓒ Weights

12. Which best fits on the line for I. B.?

  Ⓐ Exercise

  Ⓑ Essential nutrients

  Ⓒ Attitude

13. Which best fits on the line for III.?

  Ⓐ Attitude

  Ⓑ Weights

  Ⓒ Exercise

Darken the circle by the sentence that shows correct use of proofreader's marks for the underlined sentence.

14. barb ted chris and i went kamping in august

  Ⓐ barb ted chris and i went kamping in august ⊙

  Ⓑ barb ted chris and i went kamping in august ?

  Ⓒ barb ted chris and i went kamping in august ⊙

15. since i first was in line i bought the tikets

  Ⓐ since i first was in line i bought the tikets ⊙

  Ⓑ since i first was in line i bought the tikets ⊙

  Ⓒ since i first was in line i bought the tikets ⊙

Darken the circle by the sentence that is the correct revision of the underlined sentence.

16. i although understood what the ~~spanish~~ speaker was saying Ms. Cartim did not.

  Ⓐ I understood what the speaker was saying, Ms. Carlim did not.

  Ⓑ I although understood what the Spanish speaker was saying, Ms. Carlim did not.

  Ⓒ Although I understood what the speaker was saying, Ms. Carlim did not.

17. dont let me foget to stop by at the post office and mail this letter ⊙

  Ⓐ Don't let me forget to stop at the office and post mail this letter

  Ⓑ Please don't let me forget to stop at the post office and mail this letter.

  Ⓒ Please don't let me stop by the post office and mail this letter.

Language: Usage and Practice 8, SV 1419027859

Name _____ Date _____

Date _____

Dictionary: Syllables

- A **syllable** is a part of a word that is pronounced at one time.
- Dictionary entry words are divided into syllables to show how they can be divided at the end of a writing line.
- A **hyphen (-)** is placed between syllables to separate them.
  - EXAMPLE: neigh-bor-hood
- If a word has a beginning or ending syllable of only one letter, do not divide it so that one letter stands alone.
  - EXAMPLES: a-bout   bur-y

 Find each word in a dictionary. Then write each word with a hyphen between each syllable.

1. rummage _____

2. nevertheless _____

3. abominable _____

4. silhouette _____

5. biological _____

6. stationery _____

7. correspondence _____

8. character _____

9. enthusiasm _____

10. abandon _____

11. treacherous _____

12. effortless _____

13. romantic _____

14. nautical _____

15. accelerate _____

16. financial _____

17. significance _____

18. unimportant _____

19. commercial _____

20. ballerina _____

 Write two ways in which each word may be divided at the end of a writing line.

21. imagination _____ imagi-nation _____ imagina-tion _____

22. unexplainable _____

23. tropical _____

24. accomplishment _____

25. encyclopedia _____

26. librarian _____

27. astronomic _____

28. efficient _____

29. cleanliness _____

Language: Usage and Practice 8, SV 1419027859

Name _____ Date _____

Dictionary: Definitions and Parts of Speech

- A dictionary lists the **definitions** of each entry word.
- Many words have more than one definition. In such cases, the most commonly used definition is given first.
- Sometimes a definition is followed by a sentence showing a use of the entry word.
- A dictionary also tells the **part of speech** for each entry word. An abbreviation (shown below) stands for each part of speech.
- Some words may be used as more than one part of speech.
  EXAMPLE: **need** (nēd) *n.* **1.** the lack of something wanted or necessary.
  2. something wanted or necessary: *What are your basic needs for the camping trip?* *-v.* to require.

 Use the dictionary samples below to answer the questions.

pop-u-lar (pop´ yə lər) *adj.* **1.** pleasing to many people. **2.** having many friends: *Angela was voted the most popular girl in her class.* **3.** accepted by the general public: *The idea that pencils contain lead is a popular error.*

por-poise (pôr´ pəs) *n.* a warm-blooded marine mammal that is related to the dolphin.

por-tion (pôr´ shən) *n.* **1.** a part of a whole: *We spent a portion of the day at the park.* **2.** a part or share of a whole belonging to a person or a group. **3.** a helping of food served to one person. *-v.* to divide into parts or shares.

por-tray (por trā´) *v.* **1.** to draw or paint a picture of: *The artist portrayed the beautiful mountains in a painting.* **2.** to give a picture of in words; describe.

n.	noun
pron.	pronoun
v.	verb
adj.	adjective
adv.	adverb
prep.	preposition

1. Which word can be used as either a noun

   or a verb? _____

2. Which entry word has the most example

   sentences? _____

3. What part of speech is <u>porpoise</u>?

   _____

4. How many definitions are given for the word <u>porpoise</u>? _____

   for <u>portion</u>? _____   for <u>portray</u>? _____

5. Write the most commonly used definition of <u>popular</u>. _____

   _____

6. Use the first definition of <u>popular</u> in a sentence. _____

   _____

7. Write a sentence in which you use <u>portion</u> as a verb. _____

   _____

8. Use the second definition of <u>portray</u> in a sentence. _____

Language: Usage and Practice 8, SV 1419027859

Dictionary: Etymologies

> - Many dictionary entries include an **etymology**, which is the origin and development of a word.
> - An etymology is usually enclosed in brackets [ ] after the definition of the entry word.
> - The symbol < stands for the phrase "is derived from" or "comes from."
>   EXAMPLE: **razor** [Middle English *rasor* < Old French *raser*, to scrape.]
>   The word razor came into English from the Middle English word rasor, which came from the Old French word raser, which meant "to scrape."

 Use the dictionary entries below to answer the questions.

nov-el (nov´ əl) *n.* a long piece of prose fiction with a detailed plot. *-adj.* new, strange, unusual. [Old French *novelle*, unique, from Latin *novella*, new things.]
pueb-lo (pweb´ lō) *n.* **1.** a Native American dwelling made of adobe and stone that houses many people. **2. Pueblo**, a member of a Native American tribe that lives in pueblos. [Spanish *pueblo*, people or village, from Latin *populus*, people.)

punk (pungk) *n.* **1.** a dry, light, brownish substance that burns very slowly, often used to light fireworks. **2.** dry, decayed wood, used in its dry state as tinder. [Probably from Algonquin *punk*, live ashes.]
reef (rēf) *n.* part of a sail that can be rolled or folded up to reduce the amount of the sail exposed to the wind. *-v.* to roll or fold up a part of a sail. [Old Norse *rifridge*.]

1. Which word probably came from the Algonquin language? _____

2. Which languages are in the history of the word novel?

_____

3. Which word originally meant "live ashes"? _____

4. Which word comes from the word populus? _____

5. Which words have more than one language in their history? _____

_____

6. What is the meaning of the Latin word novella? _____

7. Which word is spelled the same in English as it is in Spanish?

_____

8. From what language did the Old French word novelle come?

_____

9. Which words came into English from only one earlier language? _____

_____

10. Which word comes from a word that meant "people"? _____

11. Which word comes from the word rifridge? _____

Language: Usage and Practice 8, SV 1419027859

Using the Library

> - Nonfiction books on library shelves are arranged by **call numbers.**
> - Each book is assigned a number from 000 to 999, according to its subject matter.
> - The main subject groups for call numbers are as follows:
>   - 000–099 Reference
>   - 100–199 Philosophy
>   - 200–299 Religion
>   - 300–399 Social Sciences
>   - 400–499 Languages
>   - 500–599 Science and Math
>   - 600–699 Technology
>   - 700–799 The Arts
>   - 800–899 Literature
>   - 900–999 History and Geography

✳ **Write the call number group in which you would find each book.**

1. *Australia: The Island Continent* _____

2. *Technology in a Nuclear Age* _____

3. *French: A Romance Language* _____

4. *Solving Really Hard Word Problems in Mathematics* _____

5. *Ancient Philosophy* _____

6. *World Almanac and Book of Facts* _____

7. *Artists of the 1920s* _____

8. *Funny Poems for a Rainy Day* _____

9. *Science Experiments for Teenagers* _____

10. *People in Society* _____

11. *Russian Folktales* _____

12. *Religions Around the World* _____

13. *World War I: The Complete Story* _____

14. *Encyclopaedia Britannica* _____

15. *The Social Characteristics of Pack Animals* _____

✳ **Write the titles of three of your favorite nonfiction books. Write the call number range beside each title.**

16. _____

17. _____

18. _____

Unit 6: Study Skills
Language: Usage and Practice 8, SV 1419027859

Name _____ Date _____   Date _____

Using an Encyclopedia

> - An **encyclopedia** is a reference book that contains articles on many different topics.
> - The articles are arranged alphabetically in volumes.
> - Each volume is marked to indicate which articles are inside.
> - **Guide words** are used to show the first topic on each page.
> - At the end of most articles, there is a listing of **cross-references** that suggests related topics for the reader to investigate.
> - Most encyclopedias also have an **index** of subject titles.

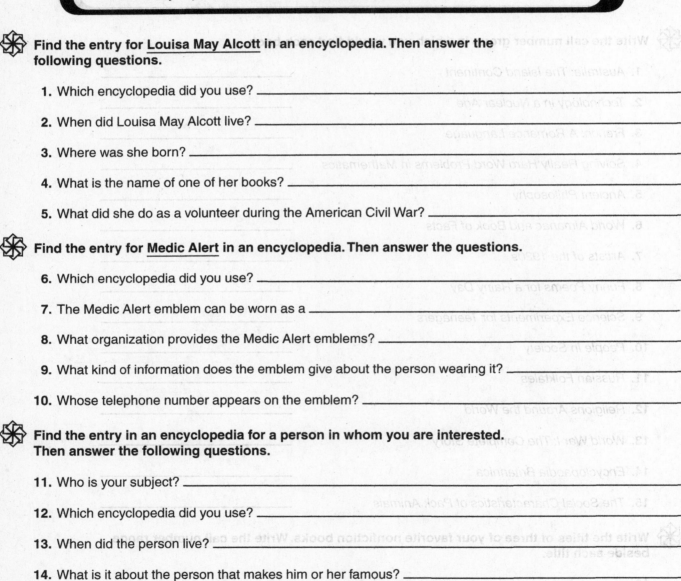

✿ **Find the entry for <u>Louisa May Alcott</u> in an encyclopedia. Then answer the following questions.**

1. Which encyclopedia did you use? _____

2. When did Louisa May Alcott live? _____

3. Where was she born? _____

4. What is the name of one of her books? _____

5. What did she do as a volunteer during the American Civil War? _____

✿ **Find the entry for <u>Medic Alert</u> in an encyclopedia. Then answer the questions.**

6. Which encyclopedia did you use? _____

7. The Medic Alert emblem can be worn as a _____

8. What organization provides the Medic Alert emblems? _____

9. What kind of information does the emblem give about the person wearing it? _____

10. Whose telephone number appears on the emblem? _____

✿ **Find the entry in an encyclopedia for a person in whom you are interested. Then answer the following questions.**

11. Who is your subject? _____

12. Which encyclopedia did you use? _____

13. When did the person live? _____

14. What is it about the person that makes him or her famous? _____

15. What cross-references are listed? _____

Name _____ Date _____

Using an Encyclopedia Index

- Most encyclopedias have an **index** of subject titles, listed in alphabetical order.
- The index shows the **volume** and the page number where an article is found. 2–10 means Volume 2, page 10.
- Some encyclopedias contain articles on many different topics.
- Some encyclopedias contain many different articles relating to a broad general topic.

 Use the sample encyclopedia index entry to answer the questions.

Index
Alligator, **1**–6; **11**–389; *see* Crocodile; Reptile
Bear, 1–35
    Black, **1**–37
    Brown, **1**–36
    Grizzly, **1**–37
    Polar, **1**–39
Cougar, 2–53; *see* Bobcat; Mountain Lion
Crocodile, 2–79; **11**–369 *see* Alligator; Reptile
Dingo, 3–94

1. In what volume would you find an article on grizzly bears? _____

2. On what pages would you find information on crocodiles? _____

3. Are all articles on bears found in the same volume? _____

4. On page 6 in Volume 1, you would find an article about what animal? _____

5. What are the cross-references for **Alligator**? _____

6. Do the words in bold show the name of the volume or the name of the animal? _____

7. Which animals have articles in two volumes? _____

8. In which volume would you expect to find information on reptiles? _____

9. Information on what animal is found in Volume 3? _____

10. If you looked under **Bobcat**, what might you expect to find as cross-references? _____

11. Information on what animal is found on page 79 in the encyclopedia? _____

12. Which of the following would be the most likely title of this encyclopedia? _____

    a. *Encyclopedia of Reptiles*   **b.** *Encyclopedia of Mammals*   **c.** *Encyclopedia of Wild Animals*

Name _____ Date _____

Using a Thesaurus

- A **thesaurus** is a reference book that writers use to find the exact words they need.
- Like a dictionary, a thesaurus lists its entry words alphabetically.
- Each entry word has a list of **synonyms**, or words that can be used in its place.
- Some thesauruses also list **antonyms** for the entry word.

  EXAMPLE: You have just written the following sentence:
  The children laughed as the tiny puppy licked their faces.
        With the help of a thesaurus, you could improve the sentence
  by replacing laughed with its more precise synonym giggled.
  The children **giggled** as the tiny puppy licked their faces.

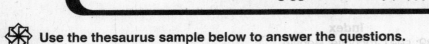 **Use the thesaurus sample below to answer the questions.**

> **move** *v. syn.* turn, budge, shift, retrieve, carry, transport, retreat, crawl, arouse, progress. *ant.* stay, stop, stabilize

1. Which is the entry word? _____

2. What are its synonyms? _____

   _____

3. Which word would you use in place of excite? _____

4. Which word would you use in place of rotate? _____

5. What are the antonyms of move? _____

6. Which word would you use in place of remain? _____

Use the synonyms of move to complete the sentences.

7. Ashley asked me if I would _____ the groceries in from the car.

8. Spot was able to _____ the golf ball from the lake.

9. Ryan's job is to _____ fruit from Michigan to other parts of the country.

10. The surfer had to _____ his weight from one leg to the other to keep his balance.

11. The instructor asked the students to _____ around in their chairs so they could see the map.

12. A baby has to _____ in order to get around.

13. We hope to _____ steadily up the mountain by climbing from ledge to ledge.

14. Robert wouldn't _____ from his favorite spot under the kitchen table.

112
Unit 6: Study Skills
Language: Usage and Practice 8, SV 1419027859

Using an Atlas

> - An **atlas** is a reference book that uses maps to organize pertinent facts about states, provinces, countries, continents, and bodies of water.
> - Additional maps show information on topography; resources, industry, and agriculture; vegetation; population; and climate.

 Use the sample atlas entry to answer the questions below.

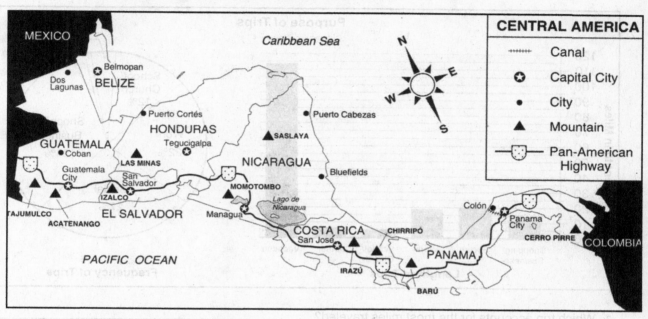

1. What part of the world is shown on this map? _____

2. How many countries make up Central America? _____

3. Which mountain is farthest west? _____

4. What major highway is shown on the map? _____

5. Which country has no mountains shown? _____

6. What is the capital of Nicaragua? _____

 Answer the questions.

7. What kind of map would you use to find out where most mining occurs in a country? _____

8. Would a topographical map show you where the most people live or where the most mountains are?

_____

9. What kind of map would you use to decide what clothes to pack for a July trip to Japan? _____

Language: Usage and Practice 8, SV 1419027859

Name _____ Date _____

Date _____ Name

Using an Almanac

- An **almanac** is a reference book that presents useful information on a wide variety of topics.
- Much of this information is in the form of tables, charts, graphs, and time lines.

 Use the sample almanac page to answer the questions.

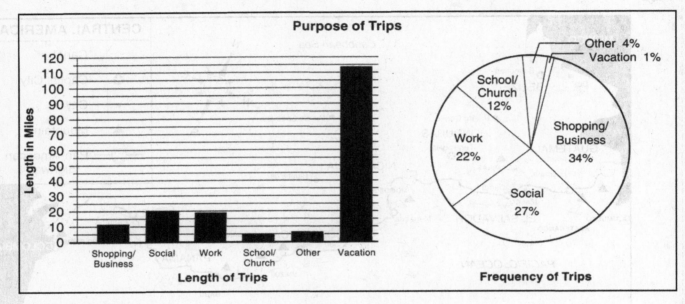

1. Which trip accounts for the most miles traveled? _____

2. What reason do people give most for taking trips? _____

3. Which three purposes together account for 60% of all trips? _____

4. Which graph shows how often people travel for a specific purpose? _____

5. Which trips are the shortest? _____

6. Do people travel farther for work or for social reasons? _____

7. Out of 100 trips, how many are made for shopping/business reasons? _____

8. What is the length of the trip least often taken? _____

9. What is the length of the trip most often taken? _____

10. Do people travel more often for school/church or for social reasons? _____

Choosing Reference Sources

- Use a **dictionary** to find definitions of words, pronunciations of words, word usage suggestions, and etymologies, or word histories.
- Use an **encyclopedia** to find articles about many different people and things. Also use an encyclopedia to find references to related subjects.
- Use a **thesaurus** to find synonyms and antonyms.
- Use the *Readers' Guide to Periodical Literature* to find magazine articles on specific subjects or by particular authors.
- Use an **atlas** to find maps and other information about geographical locations.
- Use an **almanac** to find information such as population numbers, annual rainfall, election statistics, and other specific information over a period of one year.

Write dictionary, encyclopedia, thesaurus, *Readers' Guide*, atlas, or almanac to show where you would find the following information. Some information might be found in more than one source.

_____ 1. the depth of the Indian Ocean

_____ 2. the definition of the word animosity

_____ 3. an article on parachuting

_____ 4. the usages of the word speckle

_____ 5. a synonym for the word build

_____ 6. an article on the latest development in cancer research

_____ 7. the pronunciation of the word pneumonia

_____ 8. the largest lake in Louisiana

_____ 9. facts about the life of Abraham Lincoln

_____ 10. a synonym for the word begin

_____ 11. information about John F. Kennedy's presidency

_____ 12. the origin of the word immortal

_____ 13. recent articles on home fire prevention

_____ 14. the history of the French Revolution

_____ 15. the average January temperature in Santa Fe, New Mexico

_____ 16. the states through which the Mississippi River runs

_____ 17. an antonym for the word answer

Using Reference Sources

> • Use reference sources—dictionaries, encyclopedias, the *Readers' Guide to Periodical Literature*, thesauruses, atlases, and almanacs—to find information about people, places, or things with which you are not familiar. You can also use these sources to learn more about subjects that interest you.

✵ **Follow the directions below.**

1. Find the entry for your state in one of the reference sources. Write the exact title

   of the reference source. _____

2. Write a brief summary of the information you found about your state.

   _____

   _____

   _____

   _____

   _____

✵ **Follow the directions and answer the questions.**

3. Choose a famous person you would like to know more about.

   Person's name: _____

4. List two reference sources you can use to find information about this person.

   a. _____   b. _____

5. Use one of the sources you listed above to find out when the person was born.

   Write the date of birth. _____

6. Use the appropriate reference source to find the title of the most recent article
   written about the person. Write the title of the article.

   _____

7. Use either reference source you listed in exercise 2. Find the entry for the person
   you are researching. Write a short summary of the information you found.

   _____

   _____

   _____

Language: Usage and Practice 8, SV 1419027859

Name _____ Date _____

Using Reference Sources, p. 2

 Follow the directions and answer the questions.

8. Choose a country you would like to learn more about.

   Name of country: _____

9. List four reference sources you can use to find information about this country.

   a. _____   c. _____

   b. _____   d. _____

10. Use one reference source to find the title of the most recent article written about the country. Write the title of the article.

   _____

11. Use one reference source to find out the capital of the country. Write the name

   of the capital. _____

12. Use another reference source to find out on what continent the country is located.

   Write the name of the continent. _____

13. Find the entry for the country in any one of the reference sources you listed in exercise 9. Write the exact title of the reference source.

   _____

14. Write a short summary of the information you found. Do not include information given in exercises 10, 11, or 12.

   _____

   _____

   _____

   _____

15. Find the entry for the country in one other reference source. Write the exact title

   of the reference source. _____

16. What new information did you learn about the country?

   _____

   _____

   _____

Language: Usage and Practice 8, SV 1419027859

Name _____ Date _____

Unit 6 Test

Refer to the dictionary samples to answer the questions that follow.

plunge (plunj) *v.* **1.** to throw oneself, as into water: *I plunged into the cool lake.* **2.** to enter suddenly into some condition: *The two sides plunged into war.* *-n.* the act of plunging; a dive. [Middle English *plungen,* from Old French, from Latin *plumbum,* to lead.]

pow-der (pou´ der) *n.* **1.** a dry substance of fine particles produced by crushing, grinding, etc. **2.** a specific kind of

powder: *I cleaned the soap powder from the washing machine.* *-v.* **1.** to cover with powder: *The chef powdered the rolling pin.* **2.** to make into powder. [Middle English, from Old French, from Latin *pulveris,* dust.]

prai-rie (prâr´ ē) *n.* **1.** An extensive area of flat or rolling grassland, especially the plains of central North America. [Old French *praerie,* from Latin *pratum,* meadow.]

1. Which word has one syllable?

   Ⓐ plunge   Ⓑ powder   Ⓒ prairie

2. Which word originally meant "dust"?

   Ⓐ plunge   Ⓑ powder   Ⓒ prairie

3. Which word serves as only one part of speech?

   Ⓐ plunge   Ⓑ powder   Ⓒ prairie

4. Which word has the most definitions?

   Ⓐ plunge   Ⓑ powder   Ⓒ prairie

5. Which word comes from two other languages?

   Ⓐ plunge   Ⓑ powder   Ⓒ prairie

6. Which word is not used in an example?

   Ⓐ plunge   Ⓑ powder   Ⓒ prairie

7. What does <u>plumbum</u> mean?

   Ⓐ dust   Ⓑ to lead   Ⓒ meadow

8. From how many other languages does <u>powder</u> come?

   Ⓐ two   Ⓑ three   Ⓒ four

Darken the circle by the reference source you would use to find the following information.

9. the usages of the word <u>spectacular</u>

   Ⓐ encyclopedia   Ⓒ *Readers' Guide*
   Ⓑ dictionary   Ⓓ atlas

10. information about glass manufacturing

    Ⓐ encyclopedia   Ⓒ almanac
    Ⓑ dictionary   Ⓓ atlas

11. an article written by Stella Stephens

    Ⓐ encyclopedia   Ⓒ *Readers' Guide*
    Ⓑ thesaurus   Ⓓ atlas

12. the distance from Atlanta to Savannah, Georgia

    Ⓐ encyclopedia   Ⓒ *Readers' Guide*
    Ⓑ dictionary   Ⓓ atlas

13. a recent article on medical breakthroughs

    Ⓐ encyclopedia   Ⓒ *Readers' Guide*
    Ⓑ dictionary   Ⓓ almanac

14. the elevation of Mount Everest

    Ⓐ encyclopedia   Ⓒ thesaurus
    Ⓑ dictionary   Ⓓ atlas

15. an antonym for the word <u>ornery</u>

    Ⓐ encyclopedia   Ⓒ dictionary
    Ⓑ thesaurus   Ⓓ almanac

16. the origin of the word <u>chipmunk</u>

    Ⓐ encyclopedia   Ⓒ dictionary
    Ⓑ thesaurus   Ⓓ almanac

17. the annual rainfall for Nevada

    Ⓐ encyclopedia   Ⓒ atlas
    Ⓑ dictionary   Ⓓ almanac

18. information about the Civil War

    Ⓐ encyclopedia   Ⓒ dictionary
    Ⓑ thesaurus   Ⓓ almanac

19. the pronunciation of the word <u>chimera</u>

    Ⓐ encyclopedia   Ⓒ atlas
    Ⓑ dictionary   Ⓓ almanac

Language: Usage and Practice 8, SV 1419027859

Unit 6 Test, p. 2

Darken the circle by the correct syllable division for the underlined word.

20. counselor

- Ⓐ coun-se-lor
- Ⓑ couns-e-lor
- Ⓒ co-un-se-lor
- Ⓓ coun-sel-or

21. pantomime

- Ⓐ pan-to-mime
- Ⓑ pant-o-mime
- Ⓒ pan-tom-ime
- Ⓓ pant-om-ime

Darken the circle by the item that matches the definition.

22. origin and development of a word

- Ⓐ definition
- Ⓑ part of speech
- Ⓒ etymology
- Ⓓ cross-reference

23. listing of related topics

- Ⓐ guide words
- Ⓑ cross-references
- Ⓒ part of speech
- Ⓓ etymology

Write the call number group in which you would find each book.

000–099 Reference	500–599 Science and Math
100–199 Philosophy	600–699 Technology
200–299 Religion	700–799 The Arts
300–399 Social Sciences	800–899 Literature
400–499 Languages	900–999 History and Geography

_____ **24.** *The Encyclopedia of American Holidays*

_____ **25.** *Plants of Central America*

_____ **26.** *Major Modern Religions*

_____ **27.** *The Poetry of Robert Frost*

Darken the circle by the item that matches the definition.

28. contains articles on many different topics

- Ⓐ dictionary
- Ⓒ *Readers' Guide*
- Ⓑ encyclopedia
- Ⓓ thesaurus

29. lists by author and subject all articles in many magazines

- Ⓐ almanac
- Ⓒ encyclopedia
- Ⓑ *Readers' Guide*
- Ⓓ atlas

30. used to find word usage and etymologies

- Ⓐ dictionary
- Ⓒ thesaurus
- Ⓑ almanac
- Ⓓ encyclopedia

31. presents specific information over a period of one year

- Ⓐ almanac
- Ⓒ encyclopedia
- Ⓑ atlas
- Ⓓ dictionary

Answer Key

Assessment

Pages 7–10

1. H
2. S
3. A
4. S
5. inch
6. S
7. C
8. P
9. P
10. they have
11. we will
12. generous
13. a

The words in bold should be circled.

14. E; (You); **Look**
15. IM; (You); **hand**
16. IN; you; **are**
17. D; I; **leave**
18. CS
19. CP
20. RO
21. CS
22. I
23. The word "prescription" should be labeled DO. The doctor handed Jesse the prescription [that he needed].
24. The words in bold should be circled.
   Ms. Chang, group, tour, **Jefferson Memorial**
25. The words in bold should be circled.
   uncle, **Tom Fiske**
26. past
27. future
28. present
29. future
30. are, go
31. sat, laid
32. learn, take
33. Set, sitting
34. b

The words in bold should be circled.

35. IP, **Nobody**
36. OP, **him**
37. PP, **its**
38. SP, **He**
39. **Janet and Jason**, their
40. adjective
41. adverb
42. adjective
43. adjective
44. adjective
45. adverb
46. or, **about** the complaints, **of** those people

47. Letter:
   591 W. Franklin Place
   Bent Tree, TX 78709
   Jan. 27, 2007
   Dear Ms. Coleman,
      Please know that I called you at exactly 9:15, but nobody answered the phone. I hope that you'll allow me another opportunity to tell you about my work. I have exciting news! I won the national photo contest, and my picture will be in the next issue of Parks of the World.
      I look forward to speaking with you. Please call anytime this week between 10:00 and 2:30. I'll be in one of these places: my home, my office, or my car; you have all three numbers.
             Sincerely,
             Eric Flannery

48. 3
49. 1
50. 2
51. 4
52. outlining
53. persuading
54. brainstorming
55. As the movie began, the crowd grew silent and concentrated on the action.
56. noun
57. before
58. Old French
59. hon-or
60. b
61. e
62. a
63. d
64. f
65. c
66. 500–599
67. 000–099
68. 400–499
69. 700–799
70. 800–899

Unit 1

Page 11

1.–22. Answers will vary.
23. success
24. friendly
25. courageous
26. unreliable
27. specific

Page 12

1. weight
2. sail
3. browse
4. days, inn
5. floe
6. boulder
7. pier
8. loan
9. mist
10. see
11. threw, through
12. buy, beach
13. aisle
14. principal
15. meets
16. rein
17. brake
18. There
19. flew, straight
20. allowed
21. way
22. steel
23. sale
24. fair
25. made
26. dear
27. eight
28. vane or vein
29. straight
30. through
31. sore
32. board
33. sea
34. scent or cent
35. pear or pair
36. piece
37. son
38. blew

Page 13

1. bear
2. jumper
3. saw
4. punch
5. mum
6. jar
7. ball
8. pupil
9. saw
10. ball
11. jumper
12. saw
13. mum
14. punch
15. jar
16. pupil
17. bear
18. ball

Page 14

1. rewrite
2. displeased
3. forewarned
4. impossible
5. uncertain
6. misspell
7. impatient

8.–21. Answers will vary.

Page 15

1. painter
2. tireless
3. lifelike or lifeless
4. artist
5. remarkable
6. encouragement
7. fascination
8. childhood
9. famous
10. reliable
11. glorious
12. colorless or colorful or colorist
13. occasional
14. fateful or fatal
15. comfortable or comforter or comfortless
16. hopeless or hopeful
17. believable or believer

Page 16

1.–10. Sentences will vary.
11. won't; will not
12. Let's; Let us
13. that's; that is
14. don't; do not
15. we'd; we had
16. can't; cannot
17. It's; It is
18. you're; you are
19. We'll; We will or we shall
20. doesn't; does not

Page 17

1.–12. Students should list any twelve of the following words: sandpaper, watercolor, homemade, comeback, fallout, outcome, waterfall, homeroom, outfield, backwater, backfield, roommate, paperback, playroom, underwater, playmate, understand, playback.
13.–18. Answers will vary.

Page 18

1. –; +
2. +; –
3. –; +
4. +; –
5. +; +
6. +; N
7. N; +
8. +; –
9. N; +
10. –; +
11. –; N
12. –; +

Paragraphs will vary.

Language: Usage and Practice 8, SV 1419027859

Page 19

1. J
2. C
3. A or D
4. B
5. K
6. F
7. D or A
8. H
9. E; G
10. I
11.–19. Meanings will vary.

Unit 1 Test
Pages 20–21

1. A
2. C
3. B
4. D
5. C
6. A
7. B
8. C
9. B
10. A
11. D
12. B
13. A
14. C
15. C
16. C
17. A
18. B
19. C
20. A
21. A
22. B
23. C
24. B
25. B
26. B
27. A
28. D
29. B
30. C
31. B
32. A
33. C
34. A
35. B
36. C

Unit 2
Page 22

S should precede the following sentences, and each should end with a period: 2, 5, 6, 7, 9, 11, 12, 14, 17, 18, 19, 20, 22, 23, 26, 27, 30.

Page 23

1. IN; ?
2. IN; ?
3. IM, .
4. D; .
5. E; !
6. IN; ?
7. IM; .
8. D; .
9. E; !
10. IM; .
11. D; .
12. D; .or E; !
13. IN; ?
14. IN; ?
15. IM; .
16. D; .
17. IM; .
18. D; .
19. IN; ?
20. D; .
21. IM; .
22. IN; ?
23. D; .
24. IM; .or E; !
25. IN; ?

Page 24

1. earthquake / formed
2. oceans / are
3. seasons / are
4. people / waited
5. mechanics / have
6. line / was
7. Iowa / was
8. plant / is
9. tube / was
10. year / is
11. Workers / discussed
12. Fossils / show
13. extracted, / exist
14. Shoshone / live
15. Georgia / built
16. Who / originated
17. people / watched
18. mines / were
19. steamboat / was
20. Who / brought
21. Franklin / was
22. guests / enjoyed
23. Academy / was
24. visited / were
25. Park / is
26. States / are

Page 25

Words in bold should be underlined twice.

1. meanings for that word / **cover**
2. oil / **is made**
3. highway / **winds**
4. woman in the black dress / **studied**
5. meadowlark / **builds**
6. making of ice cream / **can be**
7. stories / **have been written**
8. answer to the question / **was**
9. sentence / **should begin**
10. rotation of Earth on its axis / **causes**
11. inlet of the sea between cliffs / **is called**
12. Dutch / **cultivated**
13. mints in the United States / **are located**
14. *Poor Richard's Almanac* / **is**
15. climate of Jamaica / **attracts**
16. movie / **has been shown**
17. Acres of wheat / **rippled**
18. mechanic / **completed**
19. people in that picture / **were boarding**
20. One / **can find**
21. city of Albuquerque / **is**
22. trees / **have**
23. Sequoias, the world's tallest trees / **are found**
24. John Banister / **was**
25. trees / **hide**
26. woman / **filled**

Page 26

Words in bold should be underlined twice.

1. The movie **is playing** when?
2. I **will** never **forget** my first train trip.
3. The picture I want to buy **is** here.
4. He **has** seldom **been** ill.
5. The lights **went** out.
6. Bookcases **were** on all sides of the room.
7. You **take** the roast from the oven.
8. The speeding car **swerved** around the sharp curve.
9. You **get** out of the swimming pool.
10. You **study** for the spelling test.
11. Two children **are** in the pool.

Page 27

Words in bold should be underlined twice.

1. Lewis and Clark / **blazed**
2. The rose and the jasmine / **are**
3. Kelly and Amy / **went**
4. Chris / **swept** the floor, **dusted** the furniture, and **washed**
5. Empires / **flourish** and **decay**
6. lake / **rises** and **falls**
7. Juanita and her brother / **are**
8. Dwight D. Eisenhower and Douglas MacArthur / **were**
9. He / **turned** slowly and then **answered**
10. Museums, libraries, and art galleries / **are**
11. The computers, the desks, and the chairs / **are**
12. The plants / **grew** tall and **flowered**
13. Aseret and Teresa / **worked**
14. He / **ran** and **slid**
15. salesclerk / **added** up the numbers and **wrote**
16. Reading and baking / **are**
17. Mary / **drank** iced tea and **ate**
18. Cars and trucks / **sped**
19. Red and blue / **are**
20.–23. Sentences will vary.

Page 28

Sentences may vary.

Page 29

Words in bold should be labeled DO.

1. prevented, **accident**
2. should have, **appreciation**
3. pass, **potatoes**
4. Do, waste, **time**
5. did, keep, **coupons**
6. collects, **stamps**
7. invented, **gin**
8. Answer, **question**
9. are picking, **trophies**
10. invented, **steamboat**
11. am reading, *The Old Man and the Sea*
12. guides, **sailors**
13. gave, **alphabet**
14. should study, **history**
15. made, **cake**
16. Can, find, **object**
17. wrote, **story**
18. bought, **curios**
19. read, **minutes**
20. Did, make, **budget**
21. have, affected, **history**
22. baked, **pie**

Page 30

The words in bold should be labeled DO, and the words underlined twice should be labeled IO.

1. threw, Dave, **fastball**
2. gave, usher, **tickets**
3. handed, Chris, **prescription**
4. sold, us, **set**
5. Have, written, Andrea, **note**
6. paid, employee, **salary**
7. should teach, us, **wisdom**
8. sent, Amy, **letter**
9. show, us, **trick**
10. gave, cashier, **money**
11. gave, us, **story**
12. shows, visitors, **things**
13. gives, people, **hours**
14. give, group, **lecture**
15. has brought, us, **inventions**
16. take, Sandra, **books**
17. gave, Joanna, **plants**
18. give, me, **drink**
19. gave, flag, **name**
20. Will, give, me, **instructions**

Page 31

These clauses should be underlined.

1. We arrived late
2. The play started
3. We got one of the special programs
4. the audience applauded
5. we went for a walk
6. the walk was enjoyable

7. I noticed the moon
8. it was shining brightly
9. We walked along the lake
10. it was almost midnight
11. where some trains travel at very fast speeds
12. that we saw
13. that bears his name
14. When you respect others
15. that was perfect for him
16. who was elected without a run-off
17. that I purchased
18. When I awoke
19. who would control others
20. that can stand the test of the Sahara

Page 32
1. adjective; whose bravery won many victories
2. adjective; who reads the most books
3. adverb; because he hadn't set the alarm
4. adverb; when our team comes off the field
5. adjective; that he hears
6. adjective; that we planned
7.–10. Sentences will vary.

Pages 33–34
1. CP	9. CP	17. CX
2. CP	10. CP	18. CX
3. CX	11. CP	19. CX
4. CP	12. CX	20. CP
5. CX	13. CX	21. CX
6. CP	14. CX	22. CP
7. CX	15. CP	23. CP
8. CX	16. CP	24. CX

The words in bold should be underlined twice.
25. [The streets **are** filled with cars,] but [the sidewalks **are** empty.]
26. [Those apples **are** too sour to eat,] but [those pears **are** perfect.]
27. [She **studies** hard,] but [she **saves** some time to enjoy herself.]
28. [They **lost** track of time], so [they **were** late.]
29. [Eric **had** not **studied**,] so [he **failed** the test.]
30. [Yesterday it **rained** all day,] but [today the sun **is shining**.]

Page 35
Sentences may vary.

Page 36
Sentences will vary.

31. [I **set** the alarm to get up early,] but [I **couldn't get** up.]
32. [They **may sing** and **dance** until dawn,] but [they **will be** exhausted.]
33. [My friend **moved** to Texas,] and [I **will miss** her.]
34. [They **arrived** at the theater early,] but [there **was** still a long line.]
35. [Lisa **took** her dog to the veterinarian,] but [his office **was** closed.]
36. [The black cat **leaped**,] but [fortunately it **didn't catch** the bird.]
37. [I **found** a baseball in the bushes,] and [I **gave** it to my brother.]
38. [We **loaded** the cart with groceries,] and [we **went** to the checkout.]
39. [The stadium **was showered** with lights,] but [the stands **were** empty.]
40. [The small child **whimpered**,] and [her mother **hugged** her.]
41. [The dark clouds **rolled** in,] and [then it **began** to rain.]

The following subordinate clauses should be underlined.
42. that ... backward
43. that ... window
44. that ... outside
45. who ... star
46. who ... artist
47. that ... microwave
48. who ... music
49. because ... late
50. When ... arrives
51. because ... leg
52. When ... podium
53. If ... talk
54. that ... city
55. which ... red
56. who ... Georgia
57. when ... bat
58. When ... ball

Unit 2 Test
Pages 37–38
1. B	12. A	23. C
2. D	13. B	24. C
3. C	14. A	25. A
4. A	15. B	26. A
5. B	16. B	27. C
6. D	17. A	28. A
7. A	18. B	29. B
8. D	19. B	30. B
9. D	20. B	31. B
10. B	21. B	32. A
11. C	22. A	33. C

Unit 3
Page 39
Students should write P above the proper nouns in bold and C above the underlined common nouns.
1. **Maria**, sister
2. **Honolulu**, city, capital, **Hawaii**
3. **Rainbow Natural Bridge**, part, **Utah**
4. **The Declaration of Independence**, certificate, **United States**
5. **Abraham Lincoln**, **Edgar Allan Poe**, **Frederic Chopin**, year
6.–19. Answers will vary.
20.–25. Sentences will vary.

Page 40
1. abstract	22. collective
2. abstract	23. concrete
3. collective	24. abstract
4. abstract	25. collective
5. collective	26. collective
6. concrete	27. concrete
7. collective	28. abstract
8. collective	29. collective
9. concrete	30. concrete
10. collective	31. collective
11. abstract	32. abstract
12. collective	33. collective
13. abstract	34. concrete
14. concrete	35. collective
15. collective	36. abstract
16. abstract	37. concrete
17. concrete	38. concrete
18. collective	39. abstract
19. concrete	40. concrete
20. abstract	41. abstract
21. collective	42. abstract

Pages 41–42
1. counties
2. ponies
3. tomatoes
4. banjos
5. matches
6. windows
7. centuries
8. trenches
9. bookcases
10. videos
11. radios
12. farms
13. flies
14. heroes
15. dresses
16. boots
17. desks
18. daisies
19. mouthful
20. proof
21. 6
22. calf
23. knife
24. Jones
25. child
26. goose
27. wolf
28. roof
29. gentleman
30. editor-in-chief
31. +
32. cupful
33. trout
34. mouse
35. boxes
36. cities
37. deer
38. flashes
39. coaches
40. churches
41. potatoes
42. e's
43. O'Keefes
44. fish
45. scarves
46. n's
47. radios
48. oxen
49. pilots
50. 90's
51. women
52. i's

Page 43
1. Steve's
2. mother's
3. friends'
4. woman's
5. collector's
6. Rosa's; child's
7. Warrens'
8. vice-president's
9. mayor's
10. Tony's
11. women's
12. family's
13. day's
14. lifeguards'

Language: Usage and Practice 8, SV 1419027859

15. team's
16. children's
17. Juan's
18. Jim's
19. Pedro's
20. Chans'
21. Mark's
22. Frank's; Lindsey's
23. neighbors'
24. Masons'
25. Mexico's

Page 44

Students should circle the words in bold.

1. **Jan Matzeliger**, the ... machine,
2. **Niagara Falls**, the ... York,
3. **Harvard**, the ... States,
4. **brother** Jim
5. **Diane Feinstein**, a ... Francisco,
6. **Sears Tower**, one ... world,
7. **cousin** Liz
8. **Leontyne Price**, the ... singer,
9. **ship**, the Mayflower,
10. **dog** Jasmine
11. **Dr. Miller**, our ... physician,
12. **swimmer** Mark Spitz
13. **Fort Worth**, a ... Texas,
14. **Aunt Lee**, my ... sister,
15. **Mr. Diddon**, coach ... team,
16. **Monticello**, Jefferson's home,
17. **inventor** Thomas Edison
18. **Athens**, the ... Greece,
19. **king** Moctezuma
20. **weevil**, a small beetle,
21. **Hoover Dam**, a ... River,
22. **Antares**, a ... sun,
23. **composer** Mozart
24. **copperhead**, one ... States.
25. **Mt. McKinley**, a ... mountain,

Page 45

1. (is) scattering; scattered; (have, had, has) scattered
2. (is) expressing; expressed; (have, had, has) expressed
3. (is) painting; painted; (have, had, has) painted
4. (is) calling; called; (have, had, has) called
5. (is) cooking; cooked; (have, had, has) cooked

6. (is) observing; observed; (have, had, has) observed
7. (is) looking; looked; (have, had, has) looked
8. (is) walking; walked; (have, had, has) walked
9. (is) rambling; rambled; (have, had, has) rambled
10. (is) shouting; shouted; (have, had, has) shouted
11. (is) noticing; noticed; (have, had, has) noticed
12. (is) ordering; ordered; (have, had, has) ordered
13. (is) gazing; gazed; (have, had, has) gazed
14. (is) borrowing; borrowed; (have, had, has) borrowed
15. (is) starting; started; (have, had, has) started
16. (is) working; worked; (have, had, has) worked

Page 46

Students should underline all words listed and circle the words in bold.

1. **have** heard
2. **was** born, **has** become
3. **may have** heard
4. **had** grown
5. **had** learned
6. **was**, interested, **had** heard
7. **had** declared, **will** go, plant
8. **had** done, **had** moved
9. **should**, do, asked
10. **will** plant, was
11. **could**, remain
12. **was** traveling, pushed
13. called, **did**, have
14. **would** sleep
15.–20. Sentences will vary.

Page 47

1. brought; past
2. know; present
3. will close; future
4. will continue; future
5. has donated; present perfect
6. had told; past perfect
7. was; past
8. sings; present
9. will have paid; future perfect
10. will have been; future perfect

11. had been playing; past perfect
12. have anchored; present perfect

Pages 48–49

1. is doing; did; has done
2. is coming; came; has come
3. is eating; ate; has eaten
4. is going; went; has gone
5. is seeing; saw; has seen
6. is taking; took; has taken
7. seen
8. seen
9. taking
10. seen
11. eaten
12. gone
13. going
14. eaten
15. gone
16. taking
17. did or does
18. done
19. taking
20. come
21. eaten
22. seen
23. came or come
24. did
25. is beginning; began; has begun
26. is drinking; drank; has drunk
27. is driving; drove; has driven
28. is giving; gave; has given
29. is running; ran; has run
30. gave or is giving
31. ran or are running
32. begun
33. began
34. drunk
35. driven
36. given
37. beginning
38. run
39. ran or is running
40. began
41. given
42. beginning
43. ran or are running
44. given
45. gave
46. begun
47. drunk

48. began
49. running

Pages 50–51

1. is growing; grew; has grown
2. is knowing; knew; has known
3. is ringing; rang; has rung
4. is singing; sang; has sung
5. is speaking; spoke; has spoken
6. sung
7. grew
8. knew or knows
9. grown
10. singing
11. rung
12. grown
13. spoke
14. rang or is ringing
15. spoken
16. speaking
17. sang
18. known
19. rang
20. thrown
21. grown
22. known
23. growing
24. rang
25. spoken
26. is blowing; blew; has blown
27. is breaking; broke; has broken
28. is choosing; chose; has chosen
29. is drawing; drew; has drawn
30. is flying; flew; has flown
Answers may vary.
Suggested:
31. drawn
32. blew
33. flying
34. chose
35. chosen
36. blown
37. broke
38. broken
39. choosing
40. drew
41. broken
42. broke
43. chosen
44. broke
45. froze
46. chosen
47. broke

48. drawn
49. breaking
50. drawn

Page 52
1. is becoming; became; has become
2. is falling; fell; has fallen
3. is riding; rode; has ridden
4. is rising; rose; has risen
5. is stealing; stole; has stolen
6. is showing; showed; has shown
7. is sinking; sank; has sunk
8. is swimming; swam; has swum
9. is tearing; tore; has torn
10. is wearing; wore; has worn
11. ridden
12. risen
13. wore
14. stolen
15. riding
16. swimming
17. tore
18. sank
19. stolen
20. ridden
21. worn
22. worn
23. rose
24. risen
25. fallen

Page 53
1. imperative
2. indicative
3. subjunctive
4. imperative
5. indicative
6. indicative
7. indicative
8. subjunctive
9. imperative
10. subjunctive
11. imperative
12. imperative
13. indicative
14. subjunctive
15. indicative
16. indicative
17. subjunctive
18. imperative
19. subjunctive

Pages 54–55
1. walked; intransitive
2. is; intransitive
3. Move; transitive
4. listened; intransitive
5. wore; transitive
6. built; transitive
7. is; intransitive
8. lives; intransitive
9. appointed; transitive
10. paid; transitive
11. send; transitive
12. is; intransitive
13. drew; transitive
14. study; intransitive
15. cried; intransitive
16. made; transitive
17. ran; intransitive
18. learned; transitive
19. barked; intransitive
20. bring; transitive
21. baked; transitive
22. signed; transitive
23. repaired; transitive
24. shipped; transitive
25. may cause; transitive
26. was; intransitive
27. has; transitive
28. Explain; transitive
29. whistled; intransitive
30. blocked; transitive
31. have dropped; intransitive
32. change; transitive
33. attracts; transitive
34. was; intransitive
35. has; transitive
36. invented; transitive
37. cooked; transitive
38. discovered; transitive
39. traveled; intransitive
40. composed; transitive
41. was; intransitive
42. destroyed; transitive
43. exercises; intransitive
44. talked; intransitive
45. Have seen; transitive
46. cause; transitive
47. is studying; intransitive
48. bought; transitive

Page 56
1. was invented; passive
2. hit; active
3. was rung; passive
4. was thrown; passive
5. has bought; active
6. was announced; passive
7. blamed; active
8. were selected; passive
9. typed; active
10. stated; active
11. flopped; active
12. were written; passive
13. gave; active
14. held; active
15. has bought; active
16. was broken; passive
17. shook; active
18. was carried; passive
19. was given; passive
20. wrote; active

Page 57
1. living
2. fighting
3. Landing
4. Climbing
5. moaning
6. barking
7. Keeping
8. hanging
9. Laughing
10. Being
11. Making
12. Winning
13. pitching
14. eating
15. Playing
16. Planning
17. packing
18. howling
19. doing
20. living
21. planting; hunting; fishing
22. writing
23. skating
24. boating
25. Pressing
26. mapping
27. Swimming
28. driving

Page 58
1. to go
2. to see
3. to serve
4. To shoot
5. to walk
6. to stand; to sit; to walk; to dance
7. to use; to make
8. to get
9. to make
10. to clean
11. to be
12. to travel
13. to play
14. to rise
15. to see
16. to enter
17. to mail
18. To cook
19. to meet
20. to speak
21. to exhibit
22. To succeed
23. to see
24. to eat
25. to see
26. to have; to be
27. to receive
28. To score
29. to go
30. to paint

Page 59
1. running
2. showing
3. scampering
4. hidden
5. advancing
6. Biting
7. struck; falling
8. whispering
9. preparing
10. enjoying
11. produced
12. burdened
13. thinking
14. injured
15. expanding
16. fanned
17. shoving
18. frozen
19. playing
20. cleaned
21. Teasing
22. lifting
23. chirping
24. surviving
25. dedicated
26. Homing
27. whistling
28. Ironed
29. standing
30. loving

Page 60
1. lies
2. Lay
3. lying
4. lie
5. laid
6. laid
7. lain
8. lie
9. laid
10. lies
11. lain
12. lay
13. lies
14.–21. Sentences will vary.

Page 61
1. set
2. teaching
3. learn
4. sit
5. sifting
6. teach
7. sit
8. sat
9. teach
10. sit
11. teach; learn
12. sat
13. set
14. teach
15. set
16. taught
17. teach
18. sit
19. taught
20. taught
21. set
22. set
23. teaching
24. sitting

Page 62
1. you; my
2. you; me; I; them
3. you; me; our
4. I; you
5. We; him
6. me
7. We; they; us
8. She; me
9. She; you; me; her
10. We; them
11. we; our
12. He; their
13. She; my
14. They; us; them
15. she
16. he; you
17. She; us
18. I
19. your
20. me
21. you; our
22. I; you; my; you; it
23. I; him; my; we; her
24. they; us; their
25. Your; your
26. us; her; our

Page 63
1. its
2. It's
3. it's
4. It's
5. it's
6. It's
7. It's
8. It's; its
9. its
10. It's
11. it's
12. its
13. its
14. it's
15. its
16. It's
17. its
18. its
19. it's
20. its
21.–26. Sentences will vary.

Page 64
1. Those
2. That
3. these
4. This; that
5. those
6. that

www.harcourtschoolsupply.com
© Harcourt Achieve Inc. All rights reserved.

124

Answer Key
Language: Usage and Practice 8, SV 1419027859

7. This
8. these
9. These
10. this
11. those
12. this
13. those
14. These
15. that
16. that
17. Both
18. each
19. Several
20. some
21. Everyone
22. someone
23. Some
24. each
25. anyone
26. someone
27. Both
28. One
29. Each
30. Some
31. someone
32. Everybody

Page 65
Students should circle the words in bold.
1. **Everyone**; his or her
2. **Each**; his or her
3. **Sophia**; her
4. **I**; my
5. **members**; their
6. **women**; their
7. **Someone**; her or his
8. **each**; his or her
9. **Joanne**; her
10. **woman**; her
11. **anyone**; his or her
12. **student**; his or her
13. **I**; my
14. **woman**; her
15. **one**; his or her
16. **Joseph**; his
17. **man**; his
18. **waiters**; their
19. **student**; his or her
20. **person**; her or his
21. **man**; his
22. **woman**; her
23. **Jeff and Tom**; their
24. **Cliff**; he
25. **bird**; its
26. **Mark**; his

Page 66
Students should circle the words in bold.
1. **letter**; that
2. **Kara**; who
3. **Robert Burns**; who
4. **Sylvia**; who

5. **shop**; that
6. **farmhouse**; that
7. **pearl**; that
8. **bridge**; which
9. **animal**; that
10. **regions**; that
11. **turkey**; that
12. **story**; which
13. **person**; whom
14. **hamburgers**; that
15. **food**; that
16. **painting**; that
17. **sweater**; that
18. **one**; whom
19. **money**; that
20. **person**; who
21. **animal**; that
22. **guests**; whom
23. **file**; which
24. **artist**; whose
25. **attraction**; that
26. **writer**; whose

Page 67
1. Who
2. Who
3. Whom
4. Who
5. Who
6. Who
7. whom
8. whom
9. Who
10. whom
11. Whom
12. Whom
13. whom
14. Who
15. Whom
16. whom
17. whom
18. Whom
19. Who
20. Whom
21. Who

Page 68
1. I
2. He; I
3. that
4. he; she
5. me
6. who
7. Whom
8. me
9. whom
10. me
11. whom
12. her; me
13. she; him
14. who
15. those
16. she
17. me
18. his or her
19. me
20. Those
21. me
22. him
23. These
24. he
25. he
26. Those
27. me
28. he
29. whom
30. their
31. Who
32. she
33. his or her
34. who

Pages 69–70
1. The; old; fabulous; Greek
2. The; little; a; affectionate
3. The; weary; the; soft; green
4. The; a; magnificent; vivid
5. Every; good; good; good

6. Every; the; the; famous
7. Fleecy; white
8. every; lofty
9. many; clear; bright
10. a
11. The; beautiful; memorial; the; main; the; city
12. Cautious; dangerous
13. fertile; extensive; valuable; a; great
14. a; massive; a; broad; deep; large; black
15. The; the; a; dreary
16. a; daily
17. The; main; stately
18. a; friendly
19. The; second; the; fourth; broken
20. The; bright; colorful; the; a; wonderful
21. The; old; dusty; the
22. Yellow; green; the; curious
23. The; steaming; blueberry; the
24. An; elegant; the; black
25. the; chirping; baby
26. The; the; first
27.–35. Sentences will vary.
27. Puerto Rican
28. Irish
29. South American
30. British
31. French
32. Roman
33. Canadian
34. English
35. Russian
36.–51. Adjectives will vary.

Page 71
1. those
2. those
3. these
4. those
5. These
6. that
7. this
8. Those
9. those
10. that
11. those
12. these
13. Those
14. Those
15. that
16. these
17. this
18. Those
19. that
20. those
21. this
22. Those
23. these
24. This
25. that

Page 72
1. gentler; gentlest
2. more helpful; most helpful
3. more difficult; most difficult
4. more troublesome; most troublesome
5. higher; highest

6. more delicious; most delicious
7. more intelligent; most intelligent
8. softer; softest
9. most difficult
10. lovelier
11. more agreeable

Page 73
1. rapidly
2. very
3. Slowly; surely
4. Afterward; soundly
5. carefully; thoroughly
6. gracefully
7. Slowly; steadily
8. too; rapidly
9. always; stylishly; neatly
10. quickly; abruptly
11. seriously
12. extremely; slowly; away
13. Always; correctly; clearly
14. rapidly
15. very; quietly
16. patiently; carefully
17. everywhere
18. too; quickly
19. gently
20. here; there; everywhere
21. here; immediately
22. gaily; everywhere
23. Slowly
24. Overhead; brightly
25. thoroughly
26. speedily
27. Carefully
28. quite
29. too

Page 74
1. faster; fastest
2. more carefully; most carefully
3. more quietly; most quietly
4. slower; slowest
5. more frequently; most frequently
6. more proudly; most proudly
7. more evenly; most evenly
8. longer; longest
9. more seriously
10. highest or higher
11. more thoroughly
12. worst
13. more diligently
14. best

Page 75
1. carefully
2. calm

Language: Usage and Practice 8, SV 1419027859

3. furiously
4. patiently
5. cheerfully
6. well
7. promptly
8. respectfully
9. happy
10. legibly
11. slowly
12. happily
13. surely
14. well
15. easily
16. loudly
17. brightly
18. well
19. quickly
20. suddenly
21. cautiously
22. accurately
23. furiously
24. new
25. steadily
26. beautiful
27. courteously
28. well
29. well
30. really
31. foolishly
32. foolish
33. loudly
34. rapidly

Pages 76–77
Students should circle the words in bold.
1. **in** 1847
2. **at** the mall
3. **in** the United States; **in** 1884
4. **of** the United States; **in** Kansas
5. **for** miners; **by** Sir Humphrey Davy; **in** 1816
6. **of** North Borneo; **in** houses; **on** stilts; **in** the Brunei River
7. **by** the magician's tricks
8. **in** Canada
9. **in** New York City; **in** 1900
10. **in** the United States; **in** Jamestown; **in** 1619
11. **in** the world; **in** New York; **in** 1832
12. **of** the telephone; **in** Scotland
13. **of** the printing press
14. **of** the giant skyscrapers; **before** us
15. **in** the waves
16. **by** Thomas Jefferson

17. **upon** the quiet valley
18. **into** sleep; **by** the patter; **of** the rain
19. **beneath** the tree
20. **in** the middle; **of** the road
21. **across** the yard; **around** the tree
22. **across** the brook
23. **of** our country; **in** 1790
24. **of** violets; **into** perfume
25. **of** a person; **of** blood; **in** one minute
26. **in** 1836
27. **of** the secrets; **of** success; **of** leisure time
28. **at** this hotel
29. **in** Washington, D.C.
30. **of** iron ore; **near** the western end; **of** the Great Lakes
31. **across** this stream; **by** the recent storm
32. **of** cattle; **on** these plains
33. **in** football; **by** a team; **from** Georgia University; **in** 1896
34. **in** Chicago
35. **of** a century ago; **by** stagecoach
36. **of** stone; **in** Delhi; **in** India; **to** the skill; **of** its builders
37. **of** the evening; **by** the rumbling; **of** thunder
38. **in** a tree
39. **on** a sand dune; **in** North Carolina; **in** 1903
40. **in** Richmond; **in** 1885
41. **of** rusty nails; **in** the corner; **of** the garage
42. **near** the edge; **of** that steep cliff
43. **with** a deep snow
44. **in** the accident; **on** the expressway
45. **of** geography; **about** the features; **of** other lands
46. **of** smoke; **from** the chimney; **of** the cabin
47. **In** the distance; **of** the snowcapped peak
48. **upon** the shelf
49. **At** one time; **of** the United States
50. **between** the goal posts
51. **of** the secretary; **at** the beginning; **of** the meeting
52. **of** cheering fans; **at** the entrance
53. **toward** the ground
54. **beneath** this huge tree

55. **In** the glow; **of** the fading light; **along** the road
56. **near** the new mall
57. **in** the catalog; **in** the library
58. **through** the halls; **of** the mansion
59. **for** next year

Page 78
1. and
2. whereas
3. since
4. but
5. not only; but also
6. Neither; nor
7. and
8. Neither; nor
9. neither; nor
10. and
11. Either; or
12. and
13. Neither; nor
14. Although
15. when
16. since
17. while
18. Unless; before
19. although
20. Both; and
21. both; and
22. Unless
23. Neither; nor
24. while
25. when
26. Either; or
27. because

Page 79
1. anything
2. anything
3. any
4. anything
5. any
6. any
7. anyone
8. any
9. any
10. any
11. anything
12. anything
13. any
14. any
15. anybody
16. any
17. any
18. anything
19. any
20. any
21. anything
22. any
23. any
24. any
25. any
26. anyone
27. anybody
28. anyone
29. any

Unit 3 Test
Pages 80–81
1. B
2. C
3. C
4. A
5. B
6. A
7. C
8. B
9. B
10. C
11. A
12. A
13. D
14. B
15. A
16. C
17. B
18. A
19. C
20. B
21. C
22. A
23. C
24. A
25. A
26. A
27. B
28. A
29. B
30. C
31. B
32. B
33. B
34. A
35. C
36. D
37. B
38. C
39. B
40. B

Unit 4
Pages 82–83
Students should circle and capitalize the first letter in each of the following words:
1. Henry; Wadsworth; Longfellow; America; Evangeline; The; Courtship; Miles; Standish
2. The; Midnight; Ride; Paul; Revere; Longfellow's
3. British; *Titanic*; England; United; States
4. The; American; George; Wythe
5. He; Thomas; Jefferson; James; Monroe
6. Mississippi; River; Vicksburg; Mississippi; New; Orleans; Louisiana
7. What; Amelia
8. Robert; I
9. Vikings; Norway; Sweden; Denmark
10. The; The; Baffle Hymn; Republic; Julia; Ward; Howe
11. James; Nelson; Chicago; Illinois
12. He; Have
13. President; United; States; White; House
14. Hopi
15. Sequoia; National; Park; Sierra; Nevada; Mountains; California
16. Mayor; Jones; Senator; Small
17. Dr.; Fox
18. Ms.; Hilary; Johnson
19. Judge; Randall
20. Gov.; Dickson
21. Senator; Christopher; Larson
22. Supt.; Adams
23. Miss; Alden
24. Dr.; Tabor
25. Mr.; William; Benton
26. Maj.; Hanson
27. W.; Charles; St.
28. Orlando; FL
29. Maple Ave.; Sunset; St.
30. Mon.; Sept.
31. Gen.; T. J.; Quint
32. Memphis; TN
33. Col.; Kravitz; Dover; NH
34. Falmouth; Harbor; Dover; NH

Pages 84–85

1. ? 6. ? 11. ?
2. . 7. . 12. .
3. ? 8. . 13. .
4. . 9. ? 14. ?
5. . 10. ?

Paragraph:
Railroad?
freedom.
Railroad.
Canada.
work?
capture.
caught.
passenger."
people.
army.
camps.
soldiers.
time.
rights.
war?
person.
anyone.
Americans.

15. . or ! 23. .
16. ! 24. .
17. . 25. !
18. !; ! or . 26. !; !
19. . 27. !
20. . 28. .
21. !; ! or . 29. .
22. !

Paragraph:
fascinating?
centuries. or (!)
pets.
ago. (or !)
Egypt. (or !)
common.
toes.
incredible?
swim.
ability.
eyesight.
light.
purrs?
feel.
whiskers.
striped.
spots. (or !)
cats?

Pages 86–87

Students should place commas after words shown:

1. Anita, Travis,
2. seats,
3. game,
4. Fergas,
5. good,
6. match, clapped, cheered,
7. matches,
8. autographs,
9. name, ball,
10. much, Travis, Nick,
11. men's, women's,
12. tournament,
13. A.M.,
14. asked,
15. me,
16. said,
17. binoculars, Anita,
18. Perillo, nutritionist,
19. Students,
20. Yes,
21. First,
22. Yes,
23. Perillo,
24. OK,
25. serving, Emilio,
26. Dave, runner,
27. Class,

Paragraph: (Some punctuation may vary.)

Our neighbor, Lamont, has fruit trees on his property. "Lamont, what kinds of fruit do you grow?" I asked. "Well, I grow peaches, apricots, pears, and plums," he replied. "Wow! That's quite a variety," I said. Lamont's son, Riley, helps his dad care for the trees. "Oh, it's constant work and care," Riley said, "but the delicious results are worth the effort." After the fruit is harvested, Riley's mother, Charlotte, cans the fruit for use throughout the year. She makes preserves, and she gives them as gifts for special occasions. Charlotte sells some of her preserves to Kurt Simmons, the owner of a local shop. People come from all over the county to buy Charlotte's preserves.

Riley's aunt, Fay, grows corn, tomatoes, beans, and squash in her garden. Each year she selects her best vegetables and enters them in the fair. She has won blue ribbons, medals, and certificates for her vegetables. "Oh, I just like being outside. That's why I enjoy gardening," Fay said. Fay's specialty squash-and-tomato bread is one of the most delicious breads I have ever tasted.

Page 88

1. "Mary, ... pen?" asked Luci.
2. Luci said, "I ... uses."
3. "Well, ... ink," Mary replied.
4. "Have ... car?" asked Angelina.
5. "No," said Celia, "I ... week."
6. Angelina said, "It ... it."
7. "I ... is!" exclaimed Hector.
8. Carmelo asked, "Where ... summer?"
9. "My ... Maine," said Bradley.
10. "Tell me," Ming said, "how ... have."
11. Alison said, "The ... four."
12. "Will ... home," asked Jason, "or ... ride?"
13. I'm; can't
14. can't; Taylor's
15. I'll; nights'
16. I've; bandleader's
17. isn't; Porter's

Page 89

1. 9:10
2. you:
3. 4:00
4. types:
5. began: "Dear Sir:
6. penguins:
7. 3:30
8. Colleen is a clever teacher; she is also an inspiring one.
9. Her lectures are interesting; they are full of information.
10. She has a college degree in history; world history is her specialty.
11. She begins her classes by answering questions; she ends them by asking questions.

Page 90

1. eighty-four
2. old-fashioned
3. con-tinued
4. vice-president
5. There was a loud boom—what a fright—from the back of the theater.
6. We all turned around—I even jumped up—to see what it was.
7. It was part of the play—imagine that—meant to add suspense.
8. I'd love to see the play again—maybe next week—and bring Andrea.
9. Of Mice and Men
10. Hasta la vista
11. Little Women
12. Time

Unit 4 Test
Pages 91–92

1. A 10. C 19. D
2. C 11. C 20. A
3. D 12. B 21. C
4. C 13. D 22. B
5. A 14. D 23. D
6. C 15. A 24. B
7. C 16. B 25. A
8. D 17. C 26. D
9. A 18. C 27. B

Unit 5
Page 93
Sentences will vary.

Page 94
Students should cross out the following sentences. Students' own sentences will vary.

1. Bob's dad is an experienced carpenter.
2. Sometimes she got jobs babysitting for families with children in the swimming program.

Paragraphs will vary.

Page 95

1. Working in a fast-food restaurant is a good first job for young people.
2. A popular ice-cream parlor in our town hires young people.
3. Computers are used in fast-food restaurants.
4.–7. Topic sentences will vary.

Page 96
Paragraph:
Topic sentence: In almost every professional sport, there are far more applicants than available jobs.

Supporting Details: several hundred players are selected; only about ten percent are actually signed; this number shrinks each year; team owners want smaller and smaller teams.
1. Answers will vary.
2. Team owners want smaller and smaller teams.
3.–4. Supporting details will vary.

Page 97
1. d
2. b
3. c
4. a
5. The evening was full of surprises.
6.–7. Answers will vary.
8.–9. Answers will vary.

Page 98
1.–10. Answers will vary. Paragraphs will vary.

Page 99
Outlines will vary.

Pages 100–101
1.–3. Answers will vary.
4.–9. Paragraphs will vary.

Pages 102–103
Check that students have written the paragraph correctly. Students' proofreading and revision may vary.

Unit 5 Test
Pages 104–105
1. D   7. C   13. A
2. A   8. C   14. C
3. D   9. A   15. B
4. B   10. B   16. C
5. B   11. B   17. B
6. A   12. B

Unit 6
Page 106
1. rum-mage
2. nev-er-the-less
3. a-bom-i-na-ble
4. sil-hou-ette
5. bi-o-log-i-cal
6. sta-tion-er-y
7. cor-re-spon-dence
8. char-ac-ter
9. en-thu-si-asm
10. a-ban-don

11. treach-er-ous
12. ef-fort-less
13. ro-man-tic
14. nau-ti-cal
15. ac-cel-er-ate
16. fi-nan-cial
17. sig-nif-i-cance
18. un-im-por-tant
19. com-mer-cial
20. bal-le-ri-na
21. imag-ination; imagina-tion
22. un-explainable; unex-plainable; unexplain-able; unexplaina-ble
23. trop-ical; tropi-cal
24. ac-complishment; accom-plishment; accomplish-ment
25. en-cyclopedia; ency-clopedia; encyclo-pedia; encyclope-dia
26. li-brarian; librar-ian; librari-an
27. as-tronomic; astro-nomic; astronom-ic
28. ef-ficient; effi-cient
29. clean-liness; cleanli-ness

Page 107
1. portion
2. popular
3. noun
4. 1; 4; 2
5. pleasing to many people
6.–8. Sentences will vary.

Page 108
1. punk
2. Old French; Latin
3. punk
4. pueblo
5. novel; pueblo
6. new things
7. pueblo
8. Latin
9. punk; reef
10. pueblo
11. reef

Page 109
1. 900–999   9. 500–599
2. 600–699   10. 300–399
3. 400–499   11. 800–899
4. 500–599   12. 200–299
5. 100–199   13. 900–999
6. 000–099   14. 000–099
7. 700–799   15. 500–599
8. 800–899
16.–18. Answers will vary.

Page 110
1. Answers will vary.
2. 1832–1888
3. Germantown, PA
4. Answers will vary.
5. She was a nurse.
6. Answers will vary.
7. bracelet or necklace
8. the Medic Alert Foundation International
9. Answers may vary. Suggested: medical information
10. the foundation's
11.–15. Answers will vary.

Page 111
1. 1
2. 79, 389
3. yes
4. alligator
5. crocodile, reptile
6. animal
7. alligator and crocodile
8. 11
9. dingo
10. mountain lion, cougar
11. crocodile
12. c

Page 112
1. move
2. turn, budge, shift, retrieve, carry, transport, retreat, crawl, arouse, progress
3. arouse
4. turn
5. stay, stop, stabilize
6. stay
Answers may vary.
7. carry
8. retrieve
9. transport
10. shift
11. turn
12. crawl
13. progress
14. budge

Page 113
1. Central America
2. 7
3. Tajumulco
4. Pan-American Highway
5. Belize
6. Managua
7. an industry map
8. where the most mountains are
9. a climate map

Page 114
1. vacation
2. shopping/business
3. shopping/business, work, and other
4. circle graph
5. school/church
6. social reasons
7. 34
8. 114 miles
9. 11 miles
10. social

Page 115
1. atlas or encyclopedia
2. dictionary
3. encyclopedia or *Readers' Guide*
4. dictionary
5. thesaurus
6. *Readers' Guide*
7. dictionary
8. atlas
9. encyclopedia
10. thesaurus
11. encyclopedia or *Readers' Guide*
12. dictionary
13. *Readers' Guide*
14. encyclopedia
15. almanac
16. atlas or encyclopedia
17. thesaurus

Pages 116–117
Answers will vary.

Unit 6 Test
Page 118–119
1. A   17. D
2. B   18. A
3. C   19. B
4. B   20. D
5. C   21. A
6. C   22. C
7. B   23. B
8. B   24. 000–099
9. B   25. 500–599
10. A   26. 200–299
11. C   27. 800–899
12. D   28. B
13. C   29. B
14. D or A 30. A
15. B   31. A
16. C

Language: Usage and Practice 8, SV 1419027859